P9-DCW-604

THE SILENT ALLIANCE

Canadian Support
for
Acid Rain Controls
in the
United States
and
the Campaign
for
Additional
Electricity Exports

James M. Friedman
Michael S. McMahon

REGNERY GATEWAY • CHICAGO

Published by Regnery Gateway, Inc.
360 West Superior Street
Chicago, Illinois 60610-0890

ISBN: 0-89526-603-2

CONTENTS

SUMMARY

For several years, Canadian officials have lobbied aggressively and highly visibly to impose stringent emission controls in the United States to limit the alleged damage of the phenomenon of acid rain. During that same period, other Canadians have mounted an equally aggressive, though not as visible, marketing effort designed to increase Canadian electricity exports to the United States. Although these officials have denied any connection between the two programs, the imposition of drastic acid rain controls on United States power plants, as demanded by Canadians, would redound to Canada's competitive advantage. Recent studies and developments demonstrate just how close is the connection between the two issues.

The Canadian lobbying effort for electricity exports is rooted in Canada's need for the profits and increased employment from exploitation of its rich energy resources. Without increased sales to the United States, the Canadian nuclear power industry will probably be dismantled and then be unable to meet the Canadian electricity demand that is expected to grow at the end of this century. Additional electricity exports also allow Canada to use American financing to develop generation facilities dedicated to Canadian use once Canada's demand for electricity grows sufficiently.

These developments raise special national concerns that American lawmakers should consider carefully prior to the enactment of acid rain control legislation. First, large scale importation of Canadian electricity would create employment and income for Canadian workers at the expense of American workers. The Canadians have proposed construction of generating facilities dedicated solely for export to the United States even though there may be excess generating capacity in the United States.

Secondly, the United States would be increasing its dependence upon another foreign source of energy just as it has begun reducing its reliance upon foreign oil. Canada is not a

5

dependable long-term supplier of electricity: the Canadians have discussed terminating electricity exports to the United States in the future in order to satisfy future Canadian domestic energy demand.

Thirdly, the United States may be coerced economically into financing Canadian nuclear power plant expansion and disposing of Canadian nuclear waste in order to maintain an adequate supply of electricity. Congress should weigh these and other developments carefully before submitting to the dual Canadian lobbying efforts.

INTRODUCTION

For several years, Canadian officials have conducted an aggressive and highly visible lobbying effort to impose stringent emission controls in the United States and to limit the alleged damage of the phenomenon of acid rain. During this same period, Canadians have conducted an equally aggressive, though not as visible, marketing effort designed to increase Canadian electricity exports to the United States. Although these same officials have denied any connection between the two programs, drastic acid rain controls on U.S. power plants would redound to Canada's competitive advantage.[1]

Several new studies and developments demonstrate that the Canadian export marketing effort is more serious than previously identified. The recent urgency of Canadians to expand electricity exports coincides with Canada's increased efforts on the issue of acid rain. These studies and developments also demonstrate that the enactment of acid rain controls will enhance significantly the demand for Canadian electricity. Congress should examine carefully the implications of increased dependence upon Canadian electricity before enacting legislation that may have irreversible economic and political effects.

CANADA AND ELECTRICITY EXPORTS

The United States and Canada have been exchanging electricity since 1901 when a transmission line was constructed at Niagara Falls. Not long ago, the total amount of electricity exchanged between the two countries was still small. As recently as 1968, the United States exported more electricity to Canada than it imported.[2]

During the late 1970s, however, the electricity exchange began to grow dramatically and increasingly favored Canada.

TABLE I
Trade in Electricity[3]
(Gigawatthours)

Year	U.S. Exports	Canadian Exports	Net U.S. Imports	
1976	3,590	12,804	9,214	
1977	2,690	19,957	17,267	
1978	2,092	21,602	19,510	
1979	2,114	31,378	29,264	
1980	3,461	30,181	26,720	
1981	1,473	35,272	33,899	
1982	2,849	34,220	31,371	
1983	unavailable	unavailable	35,652	(est.)

Exports of Canadian electricity grew over 160 percent between 1976 and 1982, from 12,804 gigawatthours (GWh) to over 34,000 GWh. Net U.S. electricity imports grew 240 percent, from 9,214 GWh to 31,371 GWh [Table I].

Not unexpectedly, the dollar value of these electricity exchanges increased dramatically over the same period.

TABLE II
Gross Dollar Value of Canadian
Exports of Electricity[4]
(in million Canadian dollars)

1975	$ 104.9
1976	173.8
1977	419.3
1978	478.6
1979	738.5
1980	793.6
1981	1,143.9
1982	1,105.9
1983	1,232.0 (est.)

In the eight years from 1975 until 1982, the gross dollar value of Canadian exports of electricity rose ten-fold to over one billion dollars annually [Table II]. A recent report pre-

Total Trade In Electricity United States and Canada, 1976-1982
(In Gigawatthours)

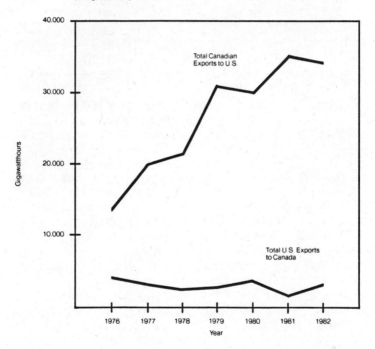

pared for the Canadian Electrical Association projects that Canada's electricity export revenues could rise to over four billion dollars by the year 2000.[5] Clearly, these exports constitute a significant amount of electricity and revenue.

Another significant aspect of these exports concerns the percentage of generation and projected demand. Estimates indicate that Hydro Quebec has enough surplus capacity to provide up to 95 percent of New York State's new demand through the year 2000.[6] The electricity Canada exported to the United States in 1981 would supply more than the annual needs of some 4.5 million residential customers in the six New England states.[7]

Electricity exports constitute an increasingly large part of total Canadian generation. In 1978, net exports of electricity represented 6 percent of net Canadian electricity generation. By 1981, it represented 9 percent.[8]

Canada plans additional electricity exports. The Power Authority of the State of New York will increase its annual imports from Quebec by 4,300 GWh and from Ontario by 3,200 GWh. The New England Power Pool could be importing up to 16,600 GWh when a proposed interconnection is expanded in 1990.[9] British Columbia Hydro recently signed a contract to sell power to the City of Seattle for $21.8 million annually.[10] The fact that the Canadian government is considering construction of generation facilities solely for export and long-term export contracts indicates the importance that Canadians place on these exports.[11]

The growth of Canada's electricity exports, particularly in terms of size and dollar value, suggests that these exports are a trade commodity and should be monitored, even if acid rain controls are not involved. The potential for huge increases in these exports as a result of American acid rain controls deserves national attention.

Canada has taken aggressive measures to build an internal consensus for additional electricity exports and then to seek such exports.

In February, 1980, the Royal Commission on Electric

Net U.S. Imports of Canadian Electricity, 1976-1983
(In Gigawatthours)

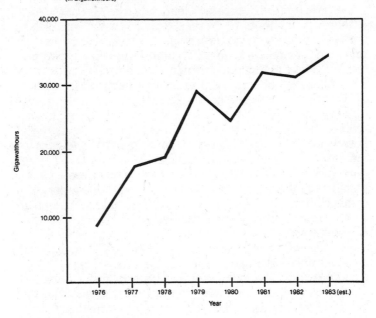

Power Planning released its five-year report on the long-range planning concepts of Ontario Hydro. The Commission noted the "potential for profitable export sales, especially sales to the United States" and stated that the "advantages of interconnections between Ontario and Michigan, and Ontario and New York cannot be overemphasized."[12] In October, 1981, Arthur Porter, former chairman of the Royal Commission, publicly urged the Province of Ontario to construct a nuclear power station dedicated to U.S. export.[13]

In 1981, Robert Bourassa, the former Premier of Quebec, extolled the benefits of increased hydro power exports to the United States.[14] Bourassa suggested that American capital could finance the then $20 billion James Bay hydro project.[15] (Robert Bourassa returned to public life on October 15, 1983, when he was reelected leader of the Liberal Party in Quebec, a position he held until after the Parti Quebecois won power in 1976.[16])

The December 1982 report by the Canadian Energy Research Institute investigated potential benefits and costs of increased electricity exports to the United States. The report recommended that "a more vigorous export policy would be in the national economic interest." The report also suggested an extensive government information campaign to convince United States utilities to purchase Canadian electricity.[17]

The then Canadian Minister of Energy Marc Lalonde travelled to the United States National Governors Conference in Afton, Oklahoma, to advertise Canada's willingness to enter into long-term contracts of up to 25 years. (Most previous contracts had tended to be short- or medium-term.) Lalonde also expressed the Canadian government's willingness to construct a nuclear generating station; most of its production would be destined for the United States.[18]

Lalonde made speeches across the United States in 1982 to promote Canadian electricity. At the New England Conference of Public Utility Commissioners, Lalonde encouraged the commissioners to approve additional imports and

Gross Dollar Value of Canada's Electricity Exports to U.S., 1976-1983
(In Hundred Million Canadian Dollars)

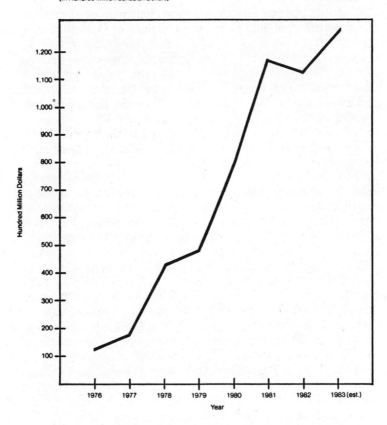

to prevent regulatory delays.[19]

When Jean Chretien succeeded Lalonde as Minister of Energy in 1983, he continued Lalonde's strong support for electricity exports and, in particular, for long-term dedicated exports of electricity.[20] More recently, Chretien announced that Canada would take even more aggressive steps to increase electricity exports to the United States. For example, Canadian utilities will be able to sign export contracts up to 30 or even 40 years in duration.[21]

In November, 1981, Ontario Energy Minister Robert Welch flew to San Francisco to promote Canadian nuclear power at the Atomic Industrial Forum meeting.[22] Also in 1981, Canada's Federal Ministry of Energy, Mines and Resources sent two officials on a tour of the eastern United States to find a market for Canadian nuclear electricity.[23]

Several proposals to sell Canadian electricity deep into the United States, away from the border areas, have received serious consideration. For example, the MANDAN project, a 500 KV transmission line running from Manitoba through North Dakota and South Dakota to Nebraska, has been under development for years.[24] These proposals do not seem far-fetched in light of British Columbia Hydro's current electricity exports to San Diego Gas & Electric.[25]

Enthusiastic Ontario Hydro officials have joined the campaign for increased exports. In September, 1981, Milan Nastich, President of Ontario Hydro, spoke before the American Public Power Association. Nastich stated that there were no technical or financial obstacles to multi-billion dollar exports and that only the "political will" was needed to resolve the issue.[26] A year later, Hugh Macaulay, Chairman of Ontario Hydro, delivered a speech weighing the benefits of additional exports.[27] Ontario Hydro has even taken a quarter-page advertisement in the *Wall Street Journal* to promote additional power sales to the United States, further demonstrating Ontario Hydro's participation in the campaign to increase electricity exports.[28]

Upon Macaulay's retirement in 1983, Nastich became acting Chairman of Ontario Hydro as well as President. He has continued the policy of expanding exports to the United States and has refused to cancel plans for construction of additional nuclear capacity. This additional capacity would add to Ontario Hydro's surplus in anticipation of sales to the United States.[29]

Quebec Hydro officials also have actively promoted increased electricity exports into the United States. To boost their U.S. energy sales, Premier Rene Levesque and several Quebec ministers attended the Conference of New England Governors and Eastern Canadian Premiers in 1982.[30] At the 1983 conference, the Canadian premiers again made a "massive energy sales pitch."[31] In October, 1982, Quebec Hydro inaugurated a new control center to manage the generation and transmission of all Quebec Hydro's electric power. This new system better enables Quebec Hydro to judge the amount of surplus power available for export.[32]

The Quebec Hydro Development Plan for 1983-85 emphasizes the promotion of exports. The plan recommends "intensified marketing" by Quebec Hydro, including daily monitoring of market trends of neighboring American utilities to "identify sales possibilities and determine the situation of Quebec Hydro's competitors."[33]

Late in 1983, Atomic Energy Canada Ltd. (AECL) began to consider forming a "trading company" to broker large blocks of power to various customers in the United States.[34] Such a trading company would provide the marketing mechanism for arrangements and contracts too large for one company to handle, as in the case of the power available from a nuclear reactor dedicated to export. This proposal marks one additional method by which Canada's governments encourage and subsidize the export of Canadian electricity.

The evidence of Canada's intentions and plans to export additional electricity to the United States is unmistakable and convincing. Analyzing Canada's incentives to export additional electricity demonstrates the seriousness of Canada's strategy.

15

Canada has at least three important incentives to export additional electricity to the United States: one, electricity exports are profitable, especially under the Canadian method of pricing; two, expansion of generating capacity would employ many Canadian workers; three, Canada can utilize American financial assistance in the development of additional generating capacity.[35]

The profitability of electricity exports is sufficient incentive by itself for Canada's vigorous steps to increase those sales. In 1982, the reported dollar value of Canadian electricity exports totalled over $1.1 billion.[36] The recent study by the Canadian Energy Research Institute projected net revenues from Canadian electricity exports and the economic impact in terms of Canadian income and employment. [Some of these results are displayed in Appendix I.] The study concluded that the total regional impact of increased power exports exceeds the impact of most other commodities.[37]

In a speech to the Canadian Nuclear Association, R.F. Brooks, Vice-Chairman of the Canadian National Energy Board, revealed National Energy Board estimates that Canadian utilities receive profits up to 39 mills per kWh on surplus hydro energy costing only a few mills per kWh. The National Energy Board also estimated that there have been profits of over 20 mills per kWh on exports of surplus coal-fired generation.[38]

Further evidence exists to establish the importance of electricity export profits to Canada:

■ Ontario Hydro received governmental approval of its proposed sale to General Public Utilities (GPU) after claiming that the Ontario economy would lose $3.5 billion if the sale was prohibited.[39] (The sale was approved by the Canadian National Energy Board, but ultimately cancelled by GPU.)

■ Quebec currently purchases power cheaply from Newfoundland under a long-term contract and then resells

16

the Newfoundland power to the United States at a significant profit. Recognizing the importance of this power, Quebec Premier Rene Levesque has threatened to sabotage any trans-Quebec power lines built to carry Newfoundland power directly to U.S. markets.[40] In return, Newfoundland has unsuccessfully attempted to thwart Quebec's electricity exports by opposing Quebec Hydro's export permits before the Canadian National Energy Board.[41]

■ Canada prices its electricity exports at the highest price competitive with United States generating alternatives.[42] Because these prices are based on the buyer's avoided costs and not the seller's cost of production, Canadian electricity exports are very profitable, particularly in the case of cheaply produced hydro power such as the Newfoundland power sold by Quebec. If American generation costs rise due to acid rain legislation, Canadian electricity prices and profits automatically will rise accordingly at no additional cost to the Canadian producers.

■ Electricity exports help increase Canada's balance of payments surplus with the United States. In April, 1983, Canada ran up a $1.99 billion (Canadian) trade surplus, a record for any month. These trade surpluses continued through 1983. With 70 percent of Canada's foreign sales coming from the United States, increasing electricity exports adds to the surplus and supports the weak Canadian dollar.[43]

Increasing electricity exports is obviously in Canada's economic interest.

A Canadian Energy Research Institute study has demonstrated that additional electricity exports would create significant new employment in Canada, and recent Canadian unemployment is particularly high.[44] [See Appendix II.]

More to the point is Canada's desperate need to find sales for its CANDU nuclear reactors. Currently, Canada's nuclear industry employs approximately 36,000 people, but nearly all nuclear plants under contract have been constructed.[45] The Canadians have been searching for additional sales as an alternative to dismantling the industry and idling these skilled employees. Prime Minister Pierre Trudeau has travelled to Mexico and South Korea in search of sales.[46] Prospective sales to Egypt have collapsed, and a sale to Romania was put on hold for several years until Canada recently agreed to an unusual barter deal to subsidize the transaction. Canada will be accepting Romanian products such as tractors, shoes, clothing, wine, and frozen fruit as payment for the nuclear reactors. The Canadian government has not announced where markets will be found for these goods.[47] The unique nature of this barter transaction highlights Canada's desperate need to secure additional sales.

With its energy surplus, Canada has no opportunity for additional domestic construction unless the electricity is dedicated for export to the United States.[48] Without additional reactor sales, all firms in this Canadian industry could be out of business by the mid-to-late 1980s.[49] Canada then would be without the expertise needed to develop the next round of CANDU generators projected for the later 1990s.[50] Milan Nastich of Ontario Hydro recently admitted that the retention of this skilled work force is one of his "big preoccupations."[51] Without continued sales, this expertise will disperse. Canada must "push hard" now for electricity exports in order to save its CANDU industry before the industry and its personnel become superfluous.[52]

The same situation prevails in hydro generation. Quebec desperately is seeking sales of electricity to the United States in order to continue the James Bay project. This project is as critical to Quebec as the CANDU industry is to Canada as a whole, if not more so. The project has generated significant construction business; termination of that construction would be a substantial blow to the Quebec economy.[53]

18

Hydro Quebec has plunged deep into debt to finance the James Bay project partially to create jobs and income for Quebec workers. However, projected interest payments on the debt now top $1 billion annually by 1986, roughly $14,000 for every Quebecer.[54] Success of the project and avoidance of financial collapse depend on increasing electricity exports to the United States.[55]

Canada is an energy rich country with much of its energy potential untapped. However, Canada has been unable to develop much of its natural resources without capital from abroad. After foreign capital assisted in the development of the oil industry in western Canada, the Canadian government adopted a National Energy Policy (NEP) in 1981. The NEP was designed to increase Canadian ownership in the oil industry, particularly the share of the federal government, at the expense of foreign interests. There are indications that the Canadians intend to use American capital to develop Canadian electrical resources and then to turn those facilities over to supply future Canadian demand.

Several sources have reported Canada's willingness to expand generating capacity for exports to the United States in exchange for assistance with costs of construction and long-term, fixed contracts to assure a steady market.[56]. Fewer sources have reported Canada's intention to use the American-financed facilities to supply future Canadian demand. Yet, the true motives behind this financing plan have surfaced on occasion. For example, as reported in the Canadian newsweekly *Macleans:*

> The new plan may prove to be a cripplingly expensive failure—or a shrewd method of getting the Americans to help pay for part of Canada's future electricity supplies. The program calls for the immediate construction of at least one eastern Canadian Candu reactor to supply electric power to utilities in the northeastern United States. At some time near the turn of the century the Americans would be cut off, and the reactor's

electrical output could be redirected to meet domestic needs.[57]

In *James Bay: Twice Over*, former Quebec Premier Robert Bourassa, a proponent of the James Bay hydro project, discussed the necessity of American investment in the James Bay project:

> We can anticipate that in order to make such investments profitable, American buyers will ask for guarantees concerning the delivery of electricity for periods ranging from ten to thirty years. *Such contracts would, however, contain clauses concerning the repatriation of energy to Quebec if needed.*[58] [emphasis added]

A recent article in *Business Week* reported that most current export contracts contain such repatriation clauses.[59]

Jean Chretien, Canada's Minister of Energy, recently confirmed the existence of this Canadian policy:

> Pre-building export facilities in advance of Canadian need is particularly attractive. It shares the benefits of power with our neighbors in the early years, and then allows Canada to recuperate (sic) an effective generating source, already partially paid for, when Canadian needs require it.[60]

Chretien announced that, if a Canadian utility signs a 30 or 40 year export contract, Canada gets the facilities constructed for that export "for free."[61]

There is precedent for Canada's use of such reversion. During the 1973-74 Middle East oil embargo, Canada refused to renew a renewable short-term electricity purchase arrangement. This action led to charges that Canada had reneged on the contract, though Canadian officials strongly deny such charges.[62] (American utility officials still refer to this case as an "unpleasant experience."[63]) Any policy which encourages greater dependence upon Canadian electricity should recognize that the Canadians intend to terminate those exports when it suits their needs.

CANADA AND ACID RAIN LEGISLATION

Over the last few years, Canadian officials have waged an expensive publicity campaign to impose acid rain controls upon American coal-fired electric plants. The costs of installing such controls have been estimated from $4–8 billion per year, with significant unemployment resulting from some control options. Before examining how the imposition of acid rain controls would benefit the Canadian electricity industry, it is useful to examine briefly Canada's lobbying efforts on acid rain and the steps Canada has taken to control its own emissions. Even a brief review reveals the disparity between Canada's preaching and practice on acid rain controls.

The Canadian government has skillfully unified most Canadians on the acid rain issue by directing their concerns to an external target. This unity is founded on the twin beliefs fostered in Canada that Canada is the innocent victim of acid rain and that the United States is responsible for all the woes Canada attributes to acid rain. Interestingly, the Canadian government began this xenophobic campaign in the late 1970s when the various debates over bilingualism, Quebec sovereignty, the National Energy Program, and the Constitution threatened to split the Canadian federation.

Until August 1983, John Roberts, Minister of the Environment, played the lead role in Canada's media campaign on acid rain.[64] He frequently travelled to the United States to give speeches on acid rain, and his continual attacks on the issue prompted one Canadian journalist to dub him "The Minister for Acid Rain."[65] Roberts' main proposal, which first appeared in February 1982, was a Canadian offer to reduce sulfur dioxide emissions by 50 percent *if* the United States also reduced its emissions by 50 percent.[66] Roberts' successor, Charles Caccia, has continued Canada's high profile on acid rain by making speeches in the United States and by holding heavily publicized meetings with Canadian provincial leaders and representatives of the U.S. government.

Canada's preaching on acid rain is well funded if not necessarily well-founded. The Ministry of the Environment has a yearly budget of one million dollars to conduct its public awareness campaign on acid rain.[67] This amount is in addition to the $650,000 increase which the Canadian government is spending on general lobbying through its embassy in the United States.[68]

The Canadians have made strong efforts to portray themselves as being in the forefront of acid rain control, thereby reinforcing the widely held belief that Canada is an "innocent victim" of acid rain. In addition to calling for a 50 percent overall reduction in sulfur dioxide emissions, Canada has announced that it will cut its allowable (not actual) sulfur dioxide emissions by 25 percent by 1990. (One wonders why the Canadians have not reduced unilaterally their sulfur dioxide emissions by the 50 percent they claim will be so beneficial.[69])

According to the Canadian position, enough scientific information is known about acid rain and has been known for some time, to justify a requirement of a 50 percent reduction in sulfur dioxide emissions. The Canadian government maintains this position despite current scientific uncertainty that a reduction in sulfur dioxide emissions in distant regions of the United States will reduce the acidity in the areas "affected" by acid rain.[70] Canadian officials dismiss any reference to the scientific uncertainty surrounding the formation, transformation, and control of acid deposition as an "information haze,"[71] and any request for further information to buttress is termed "footdragging."[72] Canadians have adopted a highly emotional rhetoric to press their campaign; they obviously aim at an emotional, rather than an objective, examination of the available scientific evidence.[73] Canada's preaching on acid rain treats the scientific rationale for a reduction program more as an article of faith than as a fact to be proven.

Canada's aggressive, emotion-laden campaign on acid rain might have some merit if the Canadian federal and provincial governments were willing to accept the same degree of controls that they wish to impose on the United States. The promise to unilaterally reduce emissions by 25% has apparently been superceded by the recent announcement that the Canadian provinces want the United States to make the first move on reducing emissions.[74] Canada merely promises to reduce sulfur dioxide in the future, and only if the United States acts first. We can examine Canada's track record of such promises in the past.

The Province of Ontario and Ontario Hydro received much praise for two scrubbers that Ontario Hydro promised to install on its coal-burning generating plants. After the termination of a large electricity export contract with General Public Utilities, Ontario Hydro cancelled its plans to install the scrubbers.[75] The Province of Ontario noisily announced that it had imposed significant nitrogen oxide emission controls on Ontario Hydro, making it a "clear leader in the forefront of nitrogen oxides pollution control." Several months later, Ontario quietly relaxed its reduction order on nitrogen oxides.[76] Ontario recently deferred a pollution control order to the Algoma Steel Corporation in order to spread the costs of necessary pollution abatement equipment over several years.[77]

The tendency to shrink from actually implementing stringent regulations apparently permeates Ontario's environmental control philosophy. Ontario has had water quality standards twice as stringent as those proposed by Canada's federal government.[78] When implementation of those standards mandated closing most Toronto area beaches, Ontario Environment Minister Andy Brandt publicly wondered whether Ontario's water bacteria guidelines "should be something other than they are."[79] Apparently, the Province of Ontario regularly promises more control than is necessary and more than it can deliver.

This pattern is not limited to the Province of Ontario. The Canadian federal government's nitrogen oxide limitations for new passenger cars is 3.1 grams per vehicle mile, allow-ing over three times the emissions of the American standard. In October 1981, a Parliamentary Subcommittee stated that it was "appalled" at this situation and recommended tightening standards.[80] As of March 1984, the standards remained the same.

Canada prides itself on a 1980 amendment to its Clean Air Act authorizing federal controls against transboundary pollution. The real purpose of this belated amendment was to allow Canada to lobby the United States Environmental Protection Agency for action against American sources under Section 115 of the U.S. Clean Air Act. Without the amendment, this action was closed to the Canadians. Ironically, the only impact of the 1980 amendment has been to subject American companies to Canadian complaints; Canada's federal government has never exercised its new authority to move against Canadian sources.

The 1981 report *Still Waters,* by the ad-hoc Parliamentary Subcommittee on Acid Rain, provided a rare self-examination of the Canadian record on acid rain. The Subcommittee noted that Canada, on a per capita basis, emits more sulfur dioxide than the United States.[81] To enable Canada to get its own house in order, the Subcommittee recommended that:

— All conversions of oil-fired electricity plants to coal use the best available emission control technology (i.e., scrubbers).

— Ontario Hydro be required to utilize best available control technology at all existing and new coal-fired plants.

— The Lingan Generating Station at Cape Breton, operated by the Nova Scotia Power Corporation, be required to utilize best available control technology.

There still are no scrubbers in Canada. In contrast, the United States had 87 scrubbers in place and 22 under construction as of early 1982.[82]

In March 1983, the Parliamentary Subcommittee regrouped to press for more action on acid rain. One member noted that the federal and provincial governments in Canada failed to adopt the committee's recommendations and that Canada's track record on acid rain was "abysmal."[83] Ordinary Canadians also have noted their government's failure to take serious steps to control emissions, even as that government criticizes the United States.[84]

Stung by these charges, the Canadian embassy and its Environmental Counselor, Bruce Jutzi, have begun circulating a draft report praising Canada's performance and its Clean Air Act. Much of this report repeats the shop-worn Canadian promises to make emission reductions in the future.

For example, Ontario projects the sulfur dioxide emissions of Ontario Hydro to decrease as follows:

Year		Sulfur Dioxide (Kilotonnes)
1982	(actual to Nov.)	460
1983		430
1984		390
1985		390
1986		390
1987		390
1988		390
1989		390
1990	and later	260

The bulk of the reductions will not occur until 1990 or later rather than being "phased in" as claimed by the Canadians. The Canadian Embassy also failed to note that Ontario Hydro's sulfur dioxide emissions *increased every year* until 1982. In 1973, Ontario Hydro's plants emitted a total of 319,000 tons of sulfur dioxide. By 1982, Ontario Hydro's plants had *increased* its sulfur dioxide emissions by nearly 60 percent to over 505,000 tons. Ontario Hydro's emissions will not fall below its 1970 levels until later this decade. Many American utilities have been emitting under their 1970 sulfur dioxide levels for several years.

The United States' record on acid rain is surprisingly good, despite Canadian and news media claims. From 1976 to 1980 midwestern states reduced their sulfur dioxide emissions dramatically.

TABLE III
Percent Changes in Selected State
Sulfur Dioxide Emissions[85]
From 1976 to 1980

Alabama	-23%
Arkansas	-31%
Illinois	-21%
Kentucky	-33%
Michigan	-36%
Minnesota	-23%
Ohio	-21%
Tennessee	-24%
West Virginia	-7%

This fact specifically refutes the Canadian charge that the American heartland has done little to control its sulfur dioxide emissions.

From 1970 to 1980, emissions of primary sulfate in the United States dipped 30 percent.[86] In 1978, Canadian emissions of primary sulfate were 30 percent the size of American emissions, even though the Canadian economy and population is roughly ten times smaller than the American economy.[87] This figure is especially important because primary sulfate, unlike sulfur dioxide, is alleged to be an immediate precursor of acid rain. On a pro rata basis, then, U.S. air pollution controls are far superior to those of Canada. The American public and industries have been bearing the costs of extensive pollution control for years.

For example, from 1973 to 1982, the Cleveland Electric Illuminating Company spent $320 million dollars for air pollution controls in capital costs alone, not including operating or maintenance costs. The impact of these expenditures was reflected, in part, in a 37 percent reduction in sulfur dioxide emissions from 1973 to 1982.[88] Moreover, there are estimates that Midwestern sulfur dioxide emissions will continue to decline significantly without additional legislation. These decreases will be due to implementation of the new source performance standards, retirement of older, inefficient plants, and development of new, cleaner generating facilities.

According to the U.S. Energy Information Administration, typical Ohio electric rates are higher than those in Vermont and Maine and roughly equal to those in the rest of New England. A mere 15 percent increase in Ohio's rate (for acid rain controls demanded by Canada) would make average Ohio rates more expensive than those in all the New England states except Connecticut.[89] While Americans pay higher costs for pollution control, Canada's Minister of Energy boasts that electricity rates across Canada average only 4¢ per kilowatthour.[90]

The United States' record on pollution control is an impressive one. There is something patently unfair about Canada's promise to reduce emissions in the future by 50 percent, but only if the United States will reduce emissions by 50 percent (or more in some proposals before Congress). Canada should take into account the sacrifices and reductions already made by the United States and the American public.

The acid rain control legislation favored by the Canadians and currently before Congress is not inexpensive. The proposals range from requiring annual sulfur dioxide reductions of 8 million tons to reductions of 12 million tons. The 12 million ton reduction most closely approximates the 50 percent reduction sought by Canadians.

Various macroeconomic studies have estimated that these proposals will cost from $4–8 billion annually.[91] The variance reflects differing assumptions as to the method for controlling sulfur dioxide emissions. The lower cost figures, favored by the Canadians and others, generally assume that

27

utilities will switch from high to low sulfur coal. Implicit in this assumption are several other assumptions that cannot be taken for granted: one, that sufficient quantities of low sulfur coal are available at a reasonable cost; two, that the boilers of these plants may burn coal with a lower sulfur content; three, that states with high sulfur coal will not require the local coal to be burned in order to protect massive employment of high sulfur coal miners.[92] The high cost studies generally assume that scrubbers will be the preferred or imposed emission control technology.[93]

To estimate the costs and rate increases attributable to acid rain legislation, the Edison Electric Institute organized a company-specific study of 24 eastern electric utilities and analyzed the effect of an 8 million ton sulfur dioxide reduction. Some of the results are provided below:

TABLE IV
Increase as Percent of 1982 Rates[94]

Utility	First Year	Five Year Levelized
Tampa Electric Company	26.4%	22.9%
The Southern Company	14.9%	12.2%
Illinois Power Company	22.3%	18.1%
Central Illinois P.S.	24.3%	20.8%
Public Service Indiana	28.0%	24.5%
Indianapolis P&L	31.5%	25.6%
Cincinnati G&E	18.4%	14.3%
Indiana & Michigan (AEP)	53.8%	34.2%
Ohio Power Co. (AEP)	51.6%	38.0%
Pennsylvania Electric	23.4%	20.3%
Wisconsin Electric Power	15.0%	12.3%

Obviously, the 12 million ton sulfur dioxide reduction requirement demanded by the Canadians would mean even higher costs and rate increases.

No matter which emissions control level and method is selected, the costs imposed upon American consumers will rise significantly, particularly those in the Midwest where most emissions reductions are targeted. This increase in costs and rates will make American coal-fired capacity less competitive with Canadian electricity imports. Canadian electricity will become more attractive to all United States utilities, even those which distribute electricity generated in coal-fired capacity.

ANALYSIS OF SUGGESTED CONSTRAINTS ON THE INCREASE OF CANADIAN ELECTRICITY EXPORTS

Various studies have identified several "constraints" on the potential increase of Canadian electricity exports. Larry Parker, an analyst in energy policy for the Congressional Research Service, undertook the most ambitious study.[95] Entitled "Acid Rain Legislation and Canadian Electricity Exports: An Unholy Alliance?," the CRS study concludes that technical, regulatory, and political constraints negate much of the advantage that acid rain legislation would give to Canadian electricity producers. The Canadian Embassy has cited this CRS Study as evidence that no link exists between Canadian electricity exports and Canada's lobbying efforts on acid rain.[96]

However, when examined in light of Canada's incentives to export electricity and its shoddy record on acid rain control, these "constraints" become illusory. The fact remains that acid rain legislation would give Canadian electricity producers a significant competitive advantage over American producers.

The most important constraint on the increase of Canadian electricity exports, one not specifically identified in the CRS Study, is the potential availability of Canadian electricity for export.[97] The CRS study analyzed the costs that acid rain legislation would place on American utilities and the resultant competitive advantage of Canadian electricity exports.[98] According to the CRS Study, however, the availability of Canadian hydro power is in doubt. Many Canadian sources anticipate that the "export window" will close sometime in the 1990s.[99]

Assuming that the export window actually will close in the next decade explains the intensive Canadian effort to impose acid rain controls in the United States as quickly as possible. The sooner acid rain controls are imposed, the more electricity Canada can export before the window closes. Since the Canadian prices are based on the buyer's avoided costs, they are designed to obtain the maximum profit possible, not the largest sales possible. In addition, given the long lead time needed for construction of new facilities, the Canadians could hope to obtain sufficient revenue from several years of sales to the United States before turning the new capacity away from the United States to meet future Canadian demand.

Even while it assumed that the supply of Canadian electricity would be limited, the CRS Study noted that decreased Canadian demand for electricity and the construction of power plants dedicated to export could increase the availability of Canadian electricity.[100] Since the release of the CRS Study, both of these forecasts have moved closer to reality, thus seriously eroding the supposed supply constraint theory.

Quebec Hydro has reduced its long-range forecast of the annual increase in Quebec's electricity demand from 6.2 percent to an average of 3.7 percent for the period 1980–1998. Quebec Hydro recognized the significance of this projected reduction: "These factors have completely changed Hydro-Quebec's position. In the medium term, *Hydro-Quebec will have large electricity surpluses for which it must rapidly find new markets.*"[101] [emphasis added] These projections took actual form when Hydro Quebec announced that its electricity exports increased 7 percent in the first half of 1983, even as its total revenue from sales within the province decreased by 1.2 percent.[102] This decreased revenue provides Hydro Quebec with additional incentive to export.

Later in 1983, Quebec Hydro further reduced its forecast growth in power demand to only 2.9 percent. Quebec Hydro also announced that its surplus of power in 1984 will reach a new record of 34 percent of the kilowatthours it will produce or is contracted to buy.[103] The utility is stepping up its efforts to export electricity in order to dispose of the surplus.

Other Canadian utilities recently have had to revise their electricity demand growth estimates downward sharply.[104] For example, the Alberta Electric Utility Planning Council revised its demand forecast from 7.6 percent growth to 4.0

percent growth for the 1982–2007 period.[105] These reductions increase surplus electricity available for export to the United States.

The potential for the construction of Canadian nuclear power plants dedicated to export has been discussed previously, but dedicated hydro power is also a distinct possibility. The James Bay project, recently delayed, could provide up to 10,000 MW of generating capacity for export.[106] American capital could accelerate or develop other projects to produce export electricity.[107]

The Canadians have continually offered long-term contracts. British Columbia Hydro, for example, entered into a 35-year agreement with the City of Seattle.[108] Any doubts over the potential supply of Canadian electricity would be removed if the costs imposed by acid rain legislation forced American utilities to bid for Canadian power.

The CRS Study did identify one actual constraint on increased exports—transmission capacity.[109] According to the study, transmission of power through several utilities ceases to be economical at some point very far from the border. Yet, British Columbia Hydro currently sells power to San Diego Gas & Electric, Pacific Power & Light, Southern California Edison, Pasadena Water & Power, and the City of Burbank.[110] Obviously, long distance transmission is not "uneconomic" *per se*. It is true that, at some point, long distance transmission of electricity ceases to be economical. However, the CRS Study's theoretical discussion of this issue did nothing to refute a claim that transmission of Canadian electricity ceases to be economic only somewhere *beyond* the southern border of the United States.

Although the CRS Study only analyzed sales of Canadian power to the Midwest, the greatest potential for increased Canadian sales is to displace oil-fired capacity in the Northeast and Mideast.[111] The Canadian competition for these sales would be the coal-fired capacity in the Midwest, which would be subject to similar wheeling and transmission distance difficulties as the Canadian utilities. Evidence of the

32

competition between midwestern and Canadian utilities is the fact that the GPU-Ontario Hydro sale was cancelled because GPU was able to obtain surplus power more cheaply from Detroit Edison.[112] The Vice-Chairman of Canada's National Energy Board recently acknowledged this competition.[113] In addition, other Midwestern utilities compete with the Canadians for the eastern markets. Ohio Edison concluded a ten-year contract to supply electricity to General Public Utilities in mid-1983. In May 1983, Ohio Edison signed a five-year contract to supply electricity to Potomac Electric Power in Washington, D.C.[114]

The Canadians do not view limited transmission capacity as a constraint, and they are aggressively marketing their electricity across the United States. Milan Nastich of Ontario Hydro has stated that the only element needed for additional sales is "political will."[115] In *Industry Week* Nastich argued that technical obstacles are not "insurmountable."[116] Increased economic incentives, such as higher costs from acid rain controls, have a way of changing political will and making long distance transmission more "economical." Fred Belaire, director of corporate economic planning for Atomic Energy Canada Ltd., the government-owned manufacturer of nuclear power plants, believes that future markets for Canadian electricity lie down both American coasts and across the American South.[117] Apparently, the Canadians are confident that, where the political will exists, a way will be found to surmount the "constraint" of limited transmission capacity.

The CRS Study briefly discussed the legal authority of the National Energy Board (NEB) to limit electricity exports through its permitting process. [Appendix V lists the exports of electrical power in 1982 licensed by the NEB.[118]] The CERI Study indicates that export licenses are issued promptly, with the entire process from application to licensing averaging one year. The CERI Study also notes that the NEB has recently received new powers designed to streamline jurisdictional disputes among the provinces. This new authority should "facilitate a more vigorous electricity export policy."[119] Given Canada's desire to export, the internal Canadian permitting process should not be viewed as a constraint.

The CRS Study also discussed the legal framework under which the National Energy Board is required to consider the environmental impacts of new facilities. Had the CRS Study reviewed the NEB's decisions in this area, it would not have considered this a "constraint."

In approving the electricity export application of the New Brunswick Electric Power Commission in 1982, the NEB found that the exports would "result in some increased incremental environmental impact and social costs from increased in-province fossil fuel generation."[120] Yet, since these costs would be "small relative to the value of the exports," the application was approved.[121] The CERI report concluded that the price that could be charged for electricity exports would be "more than sufficient" to cover environmental costs.[122]

Despite concerns expressed by members of Ontario's Parliament and several environmental groups, including the federal Ministry of the Environment, the NEB approved Ontario Hydro's application to construct a cable under Lake Erie for sales to GPU.[123] Ontario Hydro agreed to export $100 million of power in 1982 and increase its sulfur dioxide emissions by over 37,000 tons without even consulting the Ontario Ministry of the Environment.[124] Obviously, the Canadians pollute when it is profitable to do so.

This record of addressing environmental concerns and Canada's overall poor record on acid rain controls proves that environmental considerations will not be a "constraint" on Canadian electricity exports.

The CRS Study identified three criteria that an export price must meet under Canadian standards:

1. It must cover fully the cost of the electricity being exported.
2. It cannot be less than the price Canadians pay for comparable service.

3. It cannot be materially less than the least-cost alternative to the United States utility.[125]

Any proposed sale will meet the first two requirements because the Canadians do not price their electricity exports on a cost generated basis. Similarly the third requirement is of little importance since NEB officials state that a sale will usually result if a utility in the United States can save two-tenths of a cent per kWh.[126] The price usually is set at 80 percent of the buyer's avoided cost.[127] The higher the cost of U.S. generating capacity, the more likely that these requirements will be met.

The CRS study contained a lengthy discussion of Canadian acid rain requirements and concluded that those requirements would increase the cost of Canadian coal-fired capacity "in a fashion similar to that which would occur to U.S. coal-fired capacity."[128]

Since the overwhelming amount of proposed export electricity is hydro or nuclear generated, this constraint is illusory. Even in 1982, a full 60 percent of the exported electricity came from hydro generators.[129]

The CRS Study briefly discussed the federal permitting process as a "constraint" and accurately noted that permits are required only for additional construction, but not for additional sales over existing lines.[130] The General Accounting Office report, "Clear Federal Policy Guidelines Needed for Future Canadian Power Imports," was released at the same time as the CRS Study and examined this issue in depth. The GAO made these findings, among others:

1. The Department of Energy (responsible for federal permitting in this area) has no direction on how to fulfill its permitting responsibilities and, thus, has no specific set of criteria to conduct its reviews.

2. The Department of Energy's current policy is to place no prescribed limits on Canadian electricity imports.[131]

With these policies in effect, CRS cannot credibly identify federal regulatory procedures as a "constraint."

The CRS Study discussed several other federal and state laws, particularly siting requirements, with which a new

35

transmission line must comply. While these laws may constrain imports of Canadian electricity, they also apply to and constrain construction of new transmission lines from existing capacity in the United States and the construction of new capacity in the United States. Since these laws apply across the board, their impact poses no special constraint on Canadian electricity exports.

The CRS Study uses "political constraints" as a euphemism for certain groups that will oppose the export or import of Canadian electricity and may put pressure on the regulatory process to delay approvals in anticipation of preventing export sales. The export incentives discussed previously will probably check the dissent in Canada while the Canadian marketing campaign in the United States will encourage American utilities to deal with any opposition.

The most serious political constraints on Canadian electricity exports are those raised in the political battle over the imposition of acid rain controls. Since acid rain legislation would greatly enhance the competitive advantage of Canadian electricity exports, the political opposition to acid rain controls becomes *de facto* political opposition to Canadian electricity exports.

The CRS Study analyzed three ways in which restrictive acid rain legislation would increase the demand for Canadian electricity. They are:

(1) discourage use of coal-fired capacity;[132]
(2) discourage oil to coal conversions;
(3) discourage the building of new coal-fired capacity.

The CRS Study overlooked a fourth development: acid rain legislation as proposed by the Canadians would eliminate midwestern coal-fired capacity as competition for displacing U.S. oil-fired capacity in the Northeast and Mideast.[133] As noted earlier, midwestern coal-fired utilities have previously provided stiff competition to Canadian utilities. The CRS study admitted that the three developments would result from acid rain legislation and encourage the demand for Canadian electricity. However, it argued that electricity exports would not increase due to the constraints previously discussed. Since these "constraints" actually constrain nothing, *the conclusion that acid rain legislation will encourage the export of Canadian electricity is valid.*

IMPACT OF ACID RAIN LEGISLATION ON CANADIAN ELECTRICITY EXPORTS

Canada would profit by the adoption of tighter acid rain controls in the United States, and there is evidence that Canadians publicly recognize the profit in linking the two issues.

The Canadian National Energy Board considers the possibility of displacing capacity in the United States when it considers applications for export. In discussing the environmental consideratons weighed by the NEB before approving an export application for Ontario Hydro, the NEB found that:

> the export would not result in a net increase in emissions in Canada except, possibly, in 1985. It was also expected that *the export would displace U.S. generation* resulting in a decrease in emissions there.[134] [emphasis added]

Ironically, the NEB appears more concerned with reducing sulfur dioxide emissions at distant sources than with reducing emissions from the Canadian sources nearest to the "affected" areas.

After General Public Utilities cancelled the proposed purchases from Ontario Hydro, Ontario Hydro cancelled the two scrubbers it had planned. Rather than install the scrubbers to decrease emissions in the "sensitive" Province of Ontario, Hydro opted to save $240 million and continue emissions at higher levels.[135]

Arthur Porter, former chairman of the Royal Commission on Electric Power Planning, has publicly called for construction of a nuclear plant for export to the United States in order to reduce the United States' reliance on coal-fired generating stations and to turn a $150 million profit.[136]

In his book *James Bay: Twice Over,* former Quebec Premier Robert Bourassa linked Canadian acid rain efforts with the benefits of the James Bay hydro project. Bourassa stated:

> Replacing thermal energy by Quebec hydroelectricity in Quebec's neighboring areas will considerably decrease polluting fallout, namely, acid rain, in these regions as well as in Quebec.... It is not only useful to increase the capacity of interconnections, but also necessary to *study the means of increasing electricity exports so that both Quebec & Quebecers can profit without making any sacrifices.*[137] [emphasis added]

Certainly, a plan to increase American demand for Quebec power would make it easier to secure American capital for the James Bay project and make Quebec a profit without sacrifices.

Despite all protestations, Canadians do see the financial profit to be gained from increased electricity exports and the displacement of capacity in the United States.

There are several national consequences to the acceptance of increased Canadian power exports which should be evaluated carefully before acid rain legislation is adopted. First, employment and income would be lost. Since one Canadian goal is to increase Canadian employment and income, such increases must come from the United States. Every dollar sent to Canada for hydro or nuclear energy means income lost in the United States and jobs lost for American workers in mining, utility, and related industries. John Jay, President of the Utility Workers of America, has estimated that current Canadian electricity exports cost 13,000 jobs in the utility industry alone. The generating capacity displaced by those exports would have provided construction workers with 150,000 man years of work, according to the editorial in the December 1983 *Light.* Those jobs have already been transferred to Canada. There would be income effects, if not effects on unemployment, even where Canadian electricity is generated from coal mined in the United States. At a time when the unemployment in the United States is at very high levels and the United States is running a record trade deficit with Canada, any program which would export jobs and income to Canada should be carefully examined.

Accepting imports would increase U.S. dependence upon another foreign source of energy and threaten the reliability of the electric utility industry in the United States. The United States is beginning to achieve independence from foreign oil, but increasing electricity imports from Canada would be a step backward. A GAO report, "Clear Federal Policy Guidelines Needed for Future Canadian Power Imports," analyzed this issue closely. The GAO reported that three councils of the North American Electric Reliability Councils felt that the eastern United States could withstand losses of imported Canadian power up to 2,400 MW and possibly 3,700 MW during light load periods. The three councils could not withstand a 3,700 MW loss during heavy period.[138] The New England Power Pool (NEPOOL) felt that a loss of 2,000 MW alone would put a strain on the spinning reserves available within the region and the ability of neighboring systems to help during NEPOOL's shortfall.[139]

There should be serious doubt as to Canada's willingness to honor long-term commitments to supply electricity. As discussed earlier, Canada intends to terminate American exports when Canadian demand rises. Moreover, Newfoundland's legal maneuvering to break a long-term contract with its sister province Quebec casts doubt upon the willingness of the Canadian provinces to live with the long-term contracts they sign, especially with foreign customers.

There is also serious doubt as to Hydro Quebec's ability to produce reliable amounts of electricity. On December 14, 1982, a blown transformer threw the entire province of Quebec into a 12-hour blackout.[140] In 1981, energy consultant Amory Lovins wrote a memorandum to the New England utility commissioners warning about the susceptibility of

Hydro Quebec's grid system to power failures.[141] The same fears were expressed to the annual Canadian Nuclear Association conference in Montreal in June 1983.[142] The issue of overdependence and jeopardized reliability cannot be taken lightly.

A series of breakdowns in Ontario Hydro's CANDU reactors within a week in August 1983, should raise questions as to the wisdom of increasing dependence on electricity exports from Ontario. A heavy-water leak caused one breakdown at Ontario Hydro's Pickering Nuclear Generating Station. A second was caused by a leak of radioactive tritium, and a third occurred when a worker forgot to set a selector switch before a routine valve test.[143] These shutdowns cost Ontario Hydro ten to twenty thousand dollars a day in lost export sales on the spot market.[144] As of September 10, 1983, Ontario Hydro's CANDU plants suffered six breakdowns or leaks within 40 days.[145] By November 1983, five of Ontario's eleven generators were out of operation, raising questions about the future of the CANDU program. It should not be forgotten that the great Northeast blackout of 1965 was caused by a mechanical breakdown at Ontario Hydro.

A special danger exists in the large-scale purchase of Canadian nuclear power. A combination of factors make this scenario likely to occur: one, the stressed state of the U.S. nuclear industry in the United States; two, Canada's need to maintain the CANDU nuclear industry; three, the Canadian willingness to construct nuclear plants dedicated for export to the United States; four, acid rain legislation that makes coal-fired generation in the United States economically unattractive and investment in Canadian power plants attractive. The only missing factor is acid rain legislation, and the Canadian government is lobbying vigorously for such restrictions.

This situation might be beneficial, aside from the energy dependence issue, if the Canadians would be responsible for the hazards of the nuclear generation. Yet, it is likely that

41

the United States will be the depository for much of the nuclear waste generated in Canada. Already, nuclear waste from Canadian reactors is shipped to the United States.[146] Under this likely scenario, the United States would have all the hazards and expenses of nuclear generated power and its waste, yet would not have the jobs, income, and, more importantly, control of the electricity generating facilities.

. These considerations are all costs that must be weighed in the cost/benefit equation for acid rain legislation. The wide divergence between Canada's preaching and practice on acid rain and the numerous incentives to export additional electricity should cause the United States to examine critically Canada's lobbying efforts. A failure to examine carefully Canada's interests in this issue would be a poor reflection on those who would adopt acid rain legislation.

CONCLUSION

Before enacting acid rain legislation, Congress should examine the economic and national security aspects of vastly increased imports of Canadian electricity. Acid rain legislation will provide Canada's electric utilities with a competitive advantage over utilities in the United States. For this reason, Congress should consider:

(1) Enactment of a clear federal policy regulating Canadian electricity imports. These regulations should be sufficient to ensure the reliability of the electricity supply in the United States and to protect American workers and companies from losses of jobs and income.

(2) The environmental impact of massive imports, particularly the necessity to construct additional transmission capacity. The United States may become the depository for Canada's nuclear waste.

(3) The regulation of pricing of Canadian electricity imports, a possible excise tax to negate much of the competitive advantage that acid rain controls would give Canadian electricity producers.

Canada's economic interest in increasing electricity exports to the United States is very clear. Any policy or legislation that would tend to increase those exports should be critically scrutinized to determine if the economic and national interests of the United States are being protected.

APPENDIX I

INCOME IMPACT OF $1 MILLION
ELECTRICITY DEMAND
BY PROVINCE, 1980

Province	Income (thousands of 1980 dollars)	
	Provincial	Canadian
Newfoundland	950	1080
Nova Scotia	760	1040
New Brunswick	750	1030
Quebec	1110	1240
Ontario	1110	1200
Manitoba	1110	1290
Saskatchewan	990	1250
Alberta	1110	1240
British Columbia	1130	1260

(Income includes direct, indirect and induced effects.)

Source: Canadian Energy Research Institution, *Potential Benefits and Costs of Canadian Electricity Exports,* Vol I., p. 75 (December 1982).

APPENDIX II

EMPLOYMENT IMPACT OF $1 MILLION
ELECTRICITY DEMAND
BY PROVINCE, 1980

Province	Employment (man-years)	
	Provincial	Canadian
Newfoundland	7	10
Nova Scotia	16	23
New Brunswick	13	20
Quebec	13	20
Ontario	15	16
Manitoba	14	17
Saskatchewan	12	17
Alberta	12	15
British Columbia	14	16

Source: Canadian Energy Research Institute, *Potential Benefits and Costs of Canadian Electricity Exports,* Vol I., p. 75 (December, 1982).

APPENDIX III

COSTS OF COMPLYING WITH VARIOUS ACID DEPOSITION LEGISLATIVE PROPOSALS

Study	Organization	Date	Costs	Assumptions
ICF, Inc. *Forecasts of the Senate Bill/Intrastate Trading with State Protection of Local Coal.*	Environmental Protection Agency	February 28, 1983	$4.4 billion/year	Senate Bill S. 3041 (8 million ton reduction). Local Coal Protection. Intrastate trading of offsets and utility reductions permitted. Expressed in mid-1982 dollars.
ICF, Inc. *Summary of EPA's Preliminary Analysis of the Latest Senate bill to Reduce Sulfur Dioxide Emissions*	Environmental Protection Agency	September, 1982	$5.2-6.6 billion/year	Assumes a reduction of 8 million tons/SO_2 by 1995 and a cap on increases in NO_x emission rates, as called for in the July 22, 1982 Senate Committee Amendment. Assumes additional reduction to offset net increase from post-1980 new and existing sources. Expressed in Mid-1982 dollars.
DOE, Costs to reduce Sulfur Dioxide Emissions, March 1982, as supplemented by letter from James T. Bartis, DOE to Thomas Brand, EEI	Department of Energy	May 14, 1982	$5.5-7.8 billion/year	Assumes a reduction of 10 million tons/SO_2 by 1990, and additional reduction of offset net increase from post-1980 new and existing sources. No model was used. Expressed in 1982 dollars.
ICF, Inc. *Comparison of Acid Rain Analysis Undertaken by ICF for the Congressional Budget Office and Edison Electric Institute*, Draft	Edison Electric Institute	May, 1982	$6.9 billion/year	Assumes emissions cap resulting in additional control on future sources totalling a 13 million tons/SO_2 reduction by 1995. Assumes no interstate emissions trading.

COSTS OF COMPLYING WITH VARIOUS ACID DEPOSITION LEGISLATIVE PROPOSALS

Study	Organization	Date	Costs	Assumptions
ICF, Inc. *Comparison of Acid Rain Analysis Undertaken by ICF for the Congressional Budget Office and Edison Electric Institute*, Draft	Congressional Budget Office	May, 1982	$1.8 billion/year	Assumes a reduction of 5 million tons/SO$_2$ by 1990, with a 1.2 lb. SO$_2$/MMBtu emissions cap, a 0.6 lb. SO$_2$/MMBtu floor, and a 90% minimum removal above the floor. Expressed in mid-1982 dollars
ICF, Inc. *Cost and Coal Production Effects of Reducing Electrical Utility Sulfur Dioxide Emissions*	National Wildlife Federation/National Clear Air Coalition	November 14, 1981	$2.4 billion/year	Assumes 10 millions tons/SO$_2$ reduction by 1990. Assumes sufficient low cost, low sulfur coal available. Assumes interstate emissions trading. Admits reduction costs would be much greater if no trading were feasible. Source of claim that electricity rates would only rise 2%. Expressed in mid-1980 dollars.
Peabody Coal Company Fact Sheet	National Coal Association	August, 1982	$8.5 billion/year	Based on requirements of Committee amendment for 8 million tons/SO$_2$ reduction by 1995. Expressed in mid-1982 dollars.
Office of Technology Assessment, Staff Briefing Memo for the Senate Environment and Public Works Committee.	Office of Technology Assessment	June 2, 1982	$3.1 billion/year	Assumes Interstate emissions trading. Based on results of OTA model, not ICF. Assumes 1½ million ton SIP Compliance credit, giving a net 8½ million ton/SO$_2$ reduction modeled. Expressed in mid-1979 dollars.

APPENDIX IV

A Report on the Results From the Edison Electric
Institute Study of the Impacts of the Senate Committee on
Environment and Public Works Bill on Acid Rain
Legislation (S.768)

Compiled and Prepared
by
National Economic Research Associates, Inc.

for
Edison Electric Institute

June 20, 1983

EXECUTIVE SUMMARY

The Edison Electric Institute (EEI) is concerned about the accuracy of macroeconomic studies regarding the costs of acid rain control legislation. These studies have not adequately assessed numerous utility-specific considerations which could significantly increase the cost of compliance. In an effort to address these concerns, EEI developed an alternative approach to evaluate the impacts of acid rain legislation adopted in 1982 by the Senate Committee on Environment and Public Works (reintroduced in 1983 as S.768). The heart of the analysis was a study of 24 utilities in the 31 eastern states. These companies account for 3.5 million tons, or 44 percent, of the 8 million ton reduction in emissions required by the bill. As part of the effort, EEI asked the National Economic Research Associates, Inc., to review the methodology and to review, compile, and check the responses. The key results, in 1982 dollars, can be summarized as follows:

- The increases in electric rates for many utilities can be very high. One-third of the utilities reported that in the first year of compliance (1993) the increase in rates above those for the most recent years would exceed 20 percent and half reported increases above 14 percent (see Table I).
- The increases in revenue requirements per household are equally large. One-third of the utilities reported that in the first year of compliance the increases would exceed $300 per household and half indicated increases in excess of $220 (see Table 1).
- Most of the utilities reported that their compliance strategy would include retrofitting scrubbers to existing coal plants. The capital expenditures for the scrubbers and other capital equipment would exceed $15 billion for the 24 companies.

I. INTRODUCTION

During the past two years, Congress has considered a variety of legislative proposals to reduce emissions of sulfur dioxide and nitrogen oxides in the eastern United States. Two of the proposals have gained particular attention. The first is a 10 million ton sulfur dioxide reduction program introduced by Senator Mitchell and the other an 8 million ton sulfur dioxide reduction adopted last year by the Senate Committee on Environment and Public Works (currently Section 120 of S.768).

Several organizations, including the Environmental Protection Agency, Congress' Office of Technology Assessment, and the Edison Electric Institute, have conducted macroeconomic studies of the impacts of these bills. It became apparent that there were several major shortcomings in the studies. These included the failure: (1) to consider company and site-specific problems retrofitting may entail; (2) to account for important factors that will affect the choice of scrubbers as compliance options—their capital requirements and the risks associated with operating them; (3) to acknowledge that states with substantial high sulfur coal reserves may constrain utilities from fuel shifting; (4) to recognize the institutional impediments for emissions trading in the context of an emissions reduction program; and (5) to adequately reflect problems inherent in emissions variability caused by, for example, extended outages at non-fossil plants. In addition, the method of reporting costs generally understated the initial rate impacts of adding scrubbers.

In an attempt to reduce the effects of these shortcomings, EEI developed an alternative approach to assessing the economic impacts of acid rain legislation. At the heart of the analysis was a survey of a number of utilities in the East. At the request of EEI, the National Economic Research Associates, Inc. (NERA) reviewed the methodology of the survey. In addition, NERA was asked to review each response and resolve major problems that emerged from this review and to compile the results. In this report we briefly discuss: (1) the survey, (2) the basis for EEI's concern with earlier analyses; (3) the key results from the survey; and (4) the results of our review.

II. THE SURVEY

The EEI Working Group on Economic Standardization developed a methodology to estimate the company-specific impacts of acid rain legislation. The Working Group had two goals. First, it sought to provide guidelines as to how key calculations should be done and on how the bill should be interpreted so that the responses would be as comparable as possible. Second, the Group wanted the utilities to develop their own compliance strategies—scrubbing, fuel switching, etc.—based on company-specific conditions and estimates of the costs of each strategy option. As a result, the analysis is unique in that it offers insights into how individual utilities would comply with the bill.

EEI recognized that with this approach responses would not be entirely comparable. However, EEI felt that the more accurate reflection of company-specific circumstances would outweigh this disadvantage.

In an effort to ease the task of estimating compliance costs, EEI's analysis asked member companies only to consider expenditures necessitated by the bill's requirements that sulfur dioxide emissions be reduced by 8 million tons and that increases in utility sulfur dioxide emissions above 1980 levels be offset. In doing so, the analysis effectively assumed that there would be *no costs* associated with:

1. the bill's requirement that *any* post-1980 net increase in sulfur dioxide emissions from sources other than utilities be offset;
2. the bill's revocation of all sulfur dioxide State Implementation Plans relaxations granted since 1980;
3. the bill's retroactive and immediately effective ban on post-1980 increases in actual sulfur dioxide emission *rates*;

51

4. the bill's stipulation that utilities must comply with a 1.2 pound per million Btu systemwide average in states where compliance plans are not prepared or approved in a timely manner; and

5. the bill's prospective prohibition on increases in nitrogen oxide emission rates from sources other than utility coal conversions.

Since compliance with these five requirements would accelerate and enhance the rigor of the bill's reduction obligations, the legal interpretation on which EEI's analysis is based may tend to understate the costs of compliance.

The study involved 24 electric utilities in the eastern United States who responded to a questionnaire. The questionnaire consisted of four parts. In the *first* part, the utilities were asked to calculate the reduction in emissions they would be required to achieve by 1993 under the bill. The analysis assumed that the 8 million ton reduction would be apportioned among states (and sources within each state) on the basis of 1980 emissions of sulfur dioxide in excess of 1.5 pounds per million Btu. A copy of the instructions and an example of the questionnaire are given in Appendix A. The individual responses are in Appendix B. Appendix C includes an interpretation of the bill by Hunton & Williams.

The *second* part was for the utilities to describe the strategy they would use to achieve the required emissions reduction. In this part, the utilities indicated how much capacity they would retrofit with scrubbers, how much they would switch to lower sulfur fuels and how much they would retire. They were also asked to report the emissions reduction that would be achieved through each option.

In the *third* part, the utilities reported their estimates of the unit costs and other effects of each strategy option. For scrubbers, this included the capital and operating and maintenance (O&M) costs, the reduction in unit generating capability and the increase in unit outage rates. For units that would switch fuels, the utilities provided the premiums for lower sulfur coal or oil. In addition, the utilities gave the cost of replacement capacity and the annual fixed charge rates for capital expenditures.

The *last* part contained the annual cost impacts of the legislation. The impacts were reported in terms of annual revenue requirements, the increases in revenue requirements expressed as a percent of the most recent average electric rates (1981 or 1982) and the cost per household. These were reported for the first year of compliance (1993) as well as in levelized terms over the first five years (1993 through 1997). All costs were expressed in 1982 dollars.

The EEI methodology was designed to reduce the effects of the shortcomings of previous analyses (see Section III). However, the problems have not been entirely eliminated. Most utilities have not performed the detailed engineering and economic studies that would be necessary to identify and quantify all costs imposed by the legislation.

III. AREAS OF CONCERN WITH PREVIOUS STUDIES

As we have noted above, EEI had several main concerns with previous analyses of the proposed legislation—the manner in which impacts were assessed and the way in which the cost impacts were reported. In this section we discuss these concerns.

A. *Areas of Potential Bias in Estimated Impacts*

There are several specific areas in which the macroeconomic analyses may have systematically underestimated compliance costs. First, retrofitting scrubbers may entail costs far in excess of installing them at new plants. For example, at existing facilities there is often limited space available for scrubbers. This increases construction costs. Also, scrubber sludge may have to be trucked for off-site disposal. This increases the O&M costs. While industry-wide estimates of retrofit penalties have been made, the magnitude of these cost increases are site-specific and can vary widely. EEI concluded that the individual utilities can best assess these in light of their familiarity with plant-specific circumstances and their responsibilities for designing compliance plans.

Second, the ability to switch from coals of one quality to another in certain boilers may be limited unless major modifications are made. Fuel switching is an important, and often the most economic, method for achieving the emission reductions. However, if major boiler modifications are required, the economic advantages of fuel switching will be reduced, thereby raising compliance costs. Once again, in EEI's view, the need for major modifications can best be determined on a unit-by-unit basis by the utilities.

Third, political considerations may play an important role in determining the extent of fuel switching. In an effort to protect mining employment and mine-related jobs, eastern coal producing states may very well constrain fuel switching. For example, these limitations may be imposed as a matter of law, such as Section 125 of the Clean Air Act, or as a matter of policy, through technology-based control strategies. In EEI's judgment, the individual utilities will best be able to determine how such constraints will affect compliance strategies.

Fourth, the premium utilities pay for low sulfur fuels will play an important role in determining the compliance strategies that are selected and the costs of the legislation. Based on the experience of its members, EEI was concerned that the premiums for low sulfur coals projected in recent analyses of the legislation may be too low. To the extent that this is the case, the impacts of the legislation will be understated. As a result, the utilities were asked to provide their own estimates of low sulfur coal premiums and use them in estimating the impacts of the legislation on fuel costs.

Fifth, the other analyses either explicitly or implicitly assume some emissions trading will occur. This underestimates the company-by-company compliance costs for at least two reasons. It is uncertain as to the extent to which institutional barriers will limit emissions trading. Also, there will be transaction costs in trading emissions not recognized in these earlier studies.

Finally, the previous analyses apparently did not take into account the effects of events that could result in higher emissions. For example, an outage at a nuclear plant will increase fossil-fired generation and, as a result, sulfur dioxide emissions. EEI believes that utilities are best able to assess how this will affect their compliance strategies and costs. It should be noted, however, that many utilities did not take such factors into account in this study. Consequently, they have understated the cost of complying with the legislation.

B. *Reporting the Cost Impacts*

The other main area of concern was how the cost impacts were reported. In previous analyses of the legislation, the cost effects have been expressed as levelized annual costs. These were the sum of the annual capital charges, levelized over the life of the capital equipment, and the annual charges for fuel and O&M. This is certainly *one* measure of the impacts of the legislation. However, it does not reflect the large increase in electric rates that will occur in the first few years of compliance. This will occur because the legislation will raise utility capital expenditures (primarily required for retrofit scrubbers). During the first few years these capital expenses are in the rate base, the annual charges for them will be very high. These annual charges, combined with higher fuel and O&M expenses, can lead to large rate increases.

IV. SUMMARY OF RESULTS

The utilities involved in the study would account for 3.5 million tons, or 44 percent, of the 8 million ton emission reduction required by the Senate Committee bill. They indicated that a reduction of 4.5 million tons would be required to comply with the bill. The additional 1.0 million ton reduction would be necessary primarily to offset emissions growth. The responses show that the proposed legislation could have substantial impacts on electric rates. The increases in revenue requirements in the first year of compliance, 1993, expressed as a percent of the most recent rates (when all revenue requirements are expressed in 1982 dollars) were estimated to be as high as 53.8 percent. One-third of the utilities reported increases in excess of 20 percent and half of them indicated increases of at least 14 percent (see Table 1).

Households will bear, either directly or indirectly, the higher electricity costs. These increases in annual revenue requirements per household were estimated to be as high as $938 per household (in 1982 dollars).[1] One-third of the utilities reported the first year increases in costs per household will exceed $300 and half indicated increases of at least $220 per household.

In aggregate terms, the first year annual costs of the legislation will be considerable—$5.06 billion for the utilities in the study (see Table 2). A good part of this would be for the annual charge for retrofit scrubbers, although fuel switching also contributes to the cost increases. The capital expenditures for this retrofitting and for replacing capacity would be $15.30 billion (see Table 3).

V. NERA REVIEW OF EEI SURVEY METHODOLOGY

We reviewed the methodology used in the EEI survey and found it to be sound. There are, however, areas of the analysis NERA would have approached differently. But, as we note below, the overall results would not be significantly affected by these alternative approaches. In this section we touch on these briefly. First, the EEI survey relied on company-specific estimates for the premiums for low sulfur coals. Our approach would have been to rely on prices that balanced regional supplies and demands for different sulfur content coals. However, after reviewing the results, we found that some companies reported premiums lower than what we would have projected and the premiums for other companies were higher. This suggests that the key results may not be significantly affected if EEI used an approach that reflected prices determined by balancing supply and demand.

Second, in converting capital expenditures to annual charges, the EEI example, and presumably many of the utilities, used the pre-tax discount rate based on the Electric Power Research Institute's methodology. We would have recommended using the after-tax rate. This would not affect the first year impacts, and would only slightly alter the levelized effects. Moreover, this is an issue about which there is not unanimity of opinion—some analysts advocate using the pre-tax rate and others the after-tax rate.

Finally, there is the issue of replacement capacity charges. Utilities in the study generally measured the replacement capacity requirements as the reduction in net dependable capacity caused by retrofitting scrubbers. They assumed the cost of providing the replacement capacity would be the cost for a new coal plant or an average of the costs for a coal plant and a combustion turbine. We would have recommended the following approach. In planning system reliability, utilities aim to maintain a reserve margin designed to achieve a specified level of reliability. Retrofitting scrubbers reduces the unit reliability and net dependable rating. Both of these changes lower system reliability. To maintain the desired level of reliability the reserve margin will have to be increased. How this increase in reserves is achieved will vary widely depending on the amount and mix of generating capacity and the growth in electricity demand. For some companies, where projected low demand growth and excess capacity combine to create high reserves, the cost will be the O&M expense for units that will otherwise not be maintained. Some systems may be able to enter into arrangements with other utilities that have excess capacity. Other systems may have to add capacity. This can be in the form of baseload units, peakers, or a combination of the two depending on the existing capacity mix. Under these circumstances the replacement capacity costs would be higher. For most of the utilities in the study, replacement costs are a relatively small part of compliance costs. Consequently, had EEI used this approach the results would not have been fundamentally altered for these companies.

[1]The cost impacts per household are the increase in revenue requirements divided by the projected number of households for 1993. It should be noted that this will overstate the cost per household for customers of utilities with relatively large shares of industrial electricity sales. The reason is that the increased costs reflected in industrial electricity prices will be borne over broad geographical regions. At the same time, the cost per household will be understated for utilities with small shares of industrial electricity sales.

TABLE I
COST IMPACTS ON RATE PAYERS
OF SENATE BILL S.768[1]
(1982 Dollars)

Utility	Increase as Percent of 1982 Rates[2]		Increase in Revenue Requirements Per Household[3]	
	First Year[4]	Five Year Levelized	First Year[4]	Five Year Levelized
	----(Percent)----		----(Dollars)----	
	(1)	(2)	(3)	(4)
Florida Power and Light Co.	9.9%	5.0%	$180	$ 92
Tampa Electric Company	26.4	22.9	510	442
The Southern Company[5]	14.9	12.2	220	180
Illinois Power Company	22.3	18.1	344	279
Central Illinois P.S.	24.3	20.8	339	290
Public Service Indiana	28.0	24.5	478	417
Indianapolis P&L	31.5	25.6	486	394
New England Power Co.	3.9	3.9	49	49
Detroit Edison	13.2	11.8	221	198
Union Electric Company	19.8	18.1	312	285
Duke Power Company	4.9	4.3	110	96
Cincinnati G&E	18.4	14.3	275	214
Columbus & Southern Ohio (AEP)[6]	7.9	6.2	95	76
Indiana & Michigan (AEP)[7]	53.8[8]	34.2	584[8]	378
Kentucky Power Co. (AEP)	11.2	9.8	190	166
Ohio Power Co. (AEP)[7]	51.6[8]	38.0	938[8]	699
Pennsylvania Electric	23.4	20.3	285	250
Pennsylvania P&L	10.7	9.6	44	39
VEPCO	7.5	6.4	107	91
Wisconsin Power & Light	12.8	11.3	208	183
Wisconsin Electric Power	15.0	12.3	233	191

[1] Results from EEI questionnaire on cost impacts of Senate Bill S.768.
[2] Some utilities used 1981 rates, escalated to 1982 dollars, as the base.
[3] The cost impacts per household are the increase in revenue requirements divided by the projected number of households for 1993.
[4] First year is generally 1993.
[5] Georgia Power Co., Gulf Power Co., and Mississippi Power Co.
[6] One of the AEP companies, Appalachian Power Co., would achieve the required emissions reduction through the normal retirement of 725 megawatts of capacity. As a result, there would be no impact on revenue requirements.
[7] The cost impacts reflect the amortization and depreciation for capacity added to replace prematurely retired units. These charges were included only for the number of years the units would not operate as a result of the legislation.
[8] These are the costs incurred in 1995, the first year the full impacts will be incurred.

TABLE II
ANNUAL COSTS UNDER SENATE BILL S.768[1]
(1982 Dollars)

Utility	First Year[2]	Five Year Levelized
	----(Million Dollars)----	
	(1)	(2)
Florida Power & Light	$ 436	$ 223
Tampa Electric Company	210	182
The Southern Company[3]	698	572
Illinois Power Company	179	146
Central Illinois P.S.	117	100
Public Service Indiana	225	198
Indianapolis P&L	170	137
New England Power Co.	53	53
Northeast Utilities	6	6
Boston Edison Company	19[4]	19[4]
Detroit Edison	384	342
Duke Power Company	143	125
Cincinnati G&E	193	151
Columbus & Southern Ohio (AEP)[5]	55	44
Indiana & Michigan (AEP)[6]	387[7]	246
Kentucky Power Co. (AEP)	33	29
Ohio Power Co. (AEP)[6]	677[7]	499
Pennsylvania Electric	160	140
Pennsylvania P&L	166	149
VEPCO	226	191
Wisconsin Power & Light	56	49
Wisconsin Electric Power	198	162
Total for all Respondents	$5,061	$4,017

[1] Results from EEI questionnaire on cost impacts of Senate Bill S.768.
[2] First year is generally 1993.
[3] Georgia Power Co., Gulf Power Co., and Mississippi Power Co.
[4] These costs do not include the savings in revenue requirements that would be foregone by not converting to coal, which would become uneconomic under the bill.
[5] See Footnote 6 on Table 1.
[6] The cost impacts reflect the amortization and depreciation for capacity added to replace prematurely retired units. These charges were included only for the number of years the units would not operate as a result of the legislation.
[7] These are the costs incurred in 1995, the first year the full impacts will be incurred.

TABLE III
IMPACTS ON CAPITAL EXPENDITURES
OF SENATE BILL S.768[1]
(1982 Dollars)

Utility	Total Capital Expenditues	Capacity Scrubbed	Capacity Lost Due to Scrubbing	Premature Retirements
	(Million Dollars)	----------(Megawatts)----------		
	(1)	(2)	(3)	(4)
Florida P&L Co.	$ 399	1,727	26	0
Tampa Electric Company	421	1,230	25	0
The Southern Company[2]	2,307	7,160	430	0
Illinois Power Company	593	1,800	231	0
Central Illinois P.S. Co.	266	900	15	0
Public Service Indiana	600	2,346	35	0
Indianapolis P&L Co.	399	1,150	115	0
New England Power Co.	0	0	0	0
Boston Edison Company	0	0	0	0
Northeast Utilities	0	0	0	0
Detroit Edison	948	3,000	96	0
Union Electric Company	869	3,400	55	0
Duke Power Company	348	1,200	60	0
Cincinnati G&E Company	466	1,427	57	80
Columbus & Southern Ohio (AEP)[3]	183	366	37	0
Indiana & Michigan (AEP)	1,925[4]	2,210	221	900
Kentucky Power Co. (AEP)	141	390	39	0
Ohio Power Co. (AEP)	2,859[4]	3,185	318	1,080
Pennsylvania Electric Co.	222	950	29	0
Pennsylvania P&L Co.	314	1,515	61	0
VEPCO	1,189	2,843	199	0
Wisconsin P&L Co.	166	591	14	0
Wisconsin Electric Power	683	1,774	80	0
Total for all Respondents	$15,299	39,164	2,143	2,060

[1] Results from EEI questionnaire on cost impacts of Senate Bill S.768
[2] Georgia Power Co., Gulf Power Co., and Mississippi Power Co.
[3] See Footnote 6 on Table 1.
[4] Includes the capital costs for the replacement of the capacity that would be prematurely retired [see column (4)]. However, the amortization and depreciation for this capacity were included in the annual cost impacts only for the number of years the unit would not operate as a result of the legislation.

APPENDIX V

E-V
EXPORTS OF ELECTRIC ENERGY—CALENDAR YEAR 1982

| | | MEGAWATT HOURS | | | | | REPORTED DOLLAR VALUE OF EXPORT | |
| | | LICENCE AUTHORIZATION | | GROSS ENERGY EXPORTED | | | | |
EXPORTER	LICENCE NUMBER	FIRM	INTER-RUPTIBLE	FIRM	INTER-RUPTIBLE	EXCHANGE[1]	FIRM	INTER-RUPTIBLE
1 Maine and New Brunswick Electrical Power Company Limited	EL-22	250 000	–	97 178	–	–	863 339	–
	EL-23	–	25 000	–	–	–	–	–
2 Fraser Inc	EL-122	400 000	–	307 610	–	–	10 940 158	–
	EL-123	–	50 000	–	–	–	–	–
3 The New Brunswick Electric Power Commission	AO-1-EL-64	3 504 000[2]	–	594 363	–	368 741	41 536 241	–
	AO-1-EL-65[3]	–	2 190 000[2]	–	1 012 492	29 446	–	52 397 222
	AO-4-EL-66[4]	876 000	–	–	–	273 353	–	–
	EL-108	140 000	–	–	–	–	–	–
	EL-109	–	300 000	–	103 609	17 730	–	6 206 902
	EL-110	250 000	–	–	–	33 975	–	–
	EL-111	140 000	–	8 184	–	–	777 248	–
	EL-112	–	179 000	–	1 440	32	–	81 589
	EL-137	876 000	–	–	–	–	–	–
	EL-138	876 000	–	–	–	–	–	–
	EL-139	92 000	–	3 785	–	–	397 543	–
	AO-1-EL-140[3]	–	6 482 400[5]	–	822 786	2 119	–	43 560 268
	EL-141[4]	1 226 400	–	–	–	83 769	–	–
	EL-142	140 000	–	–	–	–	–	–
	EL-143	–	300 000	–	34 131	1 478	–	2 062 393
	EL-144	250 000	–	–	–	5 372	–	–
	EL-145	–	179 000	–	3 364	216	–	186 146
	ELO-169 to ELO-171	300	–	220	–	–	14 928	–

		C1	C2	C3	C4	C5	C6	C7
TOTAL NEW BRUNSWICK		–	–	1 011 340	1 977 822	39 901	54 529 457	104 494 620
4 Cedars Rapids Transmission Company Limited	ELO-150	20 000	–	–	–	–	–	–
5 Hydro-Quebec	EL-96	3 000 000	–	3 000 000	–	–	–	–
	EL-113	–	10 200 000[6]	–	5 336 139	669	120 201 732	165 046 343
	EL-131	–	320 000	–	–	–	–	–
	EL-132	131 400	–	68 009	–	–	2 746 196	–
	EL-133	–	525 000[7]	–	131 054	–	–	5 163 099
	ELO-154 to ELO-156 and ELO-158 to ELO-165	1 752	–	589	–	–	25 669	–
TOTAL QUEBEC		–	–	3 068 598	5 467 193	669	122 973 597	170 199 412
6 Ontario Hydro	EL-32	15 000	–	973	–	–	–	–
	EL-134	–	10 000 000	–	–	129 702	1 946	–
	EL-135	10 500 000	–	1 198 883	–	–	52 852 287	364 766 308
	EL-136	–	20 000 000[8]	–	9 549 837	26 498	–	–
	ELO-166	80	–	20	–	–	941	–
7 Canadian Niagara Power Company Limited	AO-1-EL-124	130 000	–	–	–	–	–	–
	AO-1-EL-125	–	380 000[9]	–	–	13 386	–	9 663 131
8 Boise Cascade Canada Ltd.	AO-3-EL-63	–	87 600	–	–	–	–	965 230
9 The Detroit and Windsor Subway Company	AO-1-ELO-152	1 250	–	1 016	–	–	–	–
10 The Canadian Transit Company	ELO-167	25	–	24	–	–	–	–

E-V (cont'd)
EXPORTS OF ELECTRIC ENERGY—CALENDAR YEAR 1982

EXPORTER	LICENCE NUMBER	MEGAWATT HOURS					REPORTED DOLLAR VALUE OF EXPORT	
		LICENCE AUTHORIZATION		GROSS ENERGY EXPORTED				
		FIRM	INTER-RUPTIBLE	FIRM	INTER-RUPTIBLE	EXCHANGE	FIRM	INTER-RUPTIBLE
11 St. Lawrence Power Company	EL-114	–	250 000	–	–	117 710	–	–
	EL-115	–	150 000	–	66 790	–	–	1 998 639
	EL-116	–	150 000	–	–	3 275	–	–
12 Dow Chemical of Canada Limited	AO-1-EL-121	–	438 000	–	18 747	–	–	862 150
TOTAL ONTARIO				1 200 916	9 935 980	31 167	52 855 174	377 279 127
13 Manitoba Hydro	EL-97	–	1 500 000	–	1 828 920	–	–	24 341 521
	EL-98	876 000	–	236 020	–	–	6 215 626	–
	EL-99	262 800	–	262 800	–	–	3 593 412	–
	EL-100	800 000	–	–	–	–	–	–
	EL-101	2 500 000	–	–	–	–	–	–
	EL-102	5 000 000	–	260	–	–	104 731	–
	EL-103	–	12 000 000	–	2 887 524	37 595	–	42 899 023
	ELO-153 and ELO-172	7 899	–	1 794	–	–	39 315	–
TOTAL MANITOBA				500 874	4 716 444	37 595	9 953 084	67 240 544
14 Saskatchewan Power	EL-117	438 000	–	33 200	–	–	1 489 420	–
	EL-119	–	876 000	–	9 065	17 335	–	78 443
	EL-120	876 000"	–	–	–	–	–	–

TOTAL SASKATCHEWAN			33 200	9 065	17 335	1 489 420	78 443
15 British Columbia Hydro and Power Authority							
EL-126	32 000	–	13 493	–	–	474 025	–
EL-127	2 000 000	–	–	–	980 589	–	–
EL-128	3 000 000	–	–	–	–	–	–
EL-129	–	525 600	–	525 600	–	–	10 434 566
EL-130	–	10 000 000	–	4 313 802	121 118	–	128 431 566
ELO-168	600	–	323	–	–	44 909	–
16 Cominco Ltd.							
EL-20	–	500 000	–	–	–	–	–
EL-104	50 000	–	–	210 993	5 673	–	5 423 912
EL-105	–	1 400 000	–	–	–	–	–
17 West Kootenay Power and Light Company							
ELO-157	50	–	28	–	–	1 017	–
TOTAL BRITISH COLUMBIA [3,4]			13 844	5 050 395	1 107 380	519 951	144 290 044
TOTAL CANADA			5 828 772	27 156 899	1 234 047	242 320 683	863 582 090

Source: Canadian National Energy Board, 1982 Annual Report

[1] Exchange is no value energy. It includes inadvertent and circulating flows equichange, storage adjustment transfer and wheeling or carrier transfer.

[2] Total exports under Licences EL-64 and EL-65 should not exceed 4 380 GW h

[3] Licence EL-65 expired 3 September 1982 and was replaced by Licence EL-140.

[4] Licence EL-66 expired 3 September 1982 and was replaced by Licence EL-141.

[5] Total exports should not exceed 6 482.4 GW h when combined with the amounts exported under Licences EL-64, EL-137, and EL-138.

[6] Total exports should not exceed 10 200 GW h when combined with the amount exported under Licence EL-96.

[7] Total exports should not exceed 525 GW h when combined with the amount exported under Licence EL-132.

[8] Total exports should not exceed 20 000 GW h when combined with the amount exported under Licence EL-135.

[9] Total exports should not exceed 380 GW h when combined with the amount exported under Licence EL-124.

[10] Total exports should not exceed 12 000 GW h when combined with the amounts exported under Licences EL-97, EL-98, EL-99, EL-100, EL-101, and EL-102.

[11] Total exports under Licences EL-119 and EL-120 should not exceed 876 GW h.

[12] Total exports should not exceed 10 000 GW h during the water year (1 October to 30 September) when combined with the amounts exported under Licences EL-128 and EL-129.

FOOTNOTES

1. In 1981, Canada's Minister of the Environment, John Roberts, called this connection "nonsense." UPI Release, October 24, 1981.
2. U.S. Department of Energy and the Ministry of Energy, Mines and Resources, Canada. *Electricity Exchanges.* Minister of Supply and Services Canada. May, 1979, p. 29.
3. U.S. Energy Information Administration, *U.S.-Canadian Electricity Trade* (November, 1982) p. 1 (data for 1976–1981) (hereinafter cited as "EIA Report"); Canadian National Energy board, *1982 Annual Report* (March 1983) pp.37-38 (data for 1982). Estimate for 1983 based upon actual January-October 1983 figures projected for a twelve-month period. Actual data for 1983 obtained by telephone inquiry to Canadian National Energy Board. A Kilowatt is one thousand watts. A Megawatt is one million watts. A Gigawatt is one billion watts. A Gigawatthour is the amount of the total energy produced by the power of one Gigawatt acting for one hour.
4. Ministry of Energy, Mines and Resources, Canada. *Electric Power in Canada.* Energy Policy Sector, 1979, p. 26 (data for 1975–77). Canadian National Energy Board, *1982 Annual Report,* p. 40 (data for 1978–82). For 1983 estimate, see previous footnote.
5. Canadian Energy Research Institute, *Potential Benefits and Costs of Canadian Electricity Exports,* December, 1982, Vol. I, p. xiv (hereinafter cited as "CERI Report").
6. Holmes, P.A. "Pushing to Peddle Canadian Power," *Fortune,* September 20, 1982, citing Richard Pouliot of Quebec's Ministry of Energy.
7. General Accounting Office, "Clear Federal Policy Guidelines Needed for Future Canadian Power Imports." (September 20, 1982) p. 1 (hereinafter cited as "GAO Report").

8. Ministry of Energy, Mines and Resources, Canada. *Electric Power in Canada,* 1979, p. 24; Canadian National Energy Board, *1982 Annual Report,* p.38.

9. *GAO Report, supra* note 7, p. 4.

10. "B.C. nets huge sale in hydro deal with U.S.," *Toronto Star,* April 15, 1983, p. A9.

11. Address by Marc Lalonde, Canadian Minister of Energy, Mines and Resources, to the National Governors' Conference, Afton, Oklahoma, August 9, 1982; "Ottawa wants to boost electricity sales to U.S.," *Toronto Star,* October 19, 1983, p.B4. The statements of elected officials are particularly useful indications of the plans of the Canadian electric industry because, unlike most American utilities, Canadian utilities are governmentally owned.

12. Royal Commission on Electric Power Planning, *Concepts, Conclusions and Recommendations,* vol. I, pp. 106, 148–49 (February, 1980).

13. "Build nuclear plant to sell U.S. power, Ontario told," *Toronto Star,* October 25, 1981, p. A22.

14. Robert Bourassa, *James Bay: Twice Over* (March, 1981). Excerpts translated by Brigette Boesenberg from book published in French (hereinafter cited as "James Bay").

15. *Id.*

16. "Bourassa's back to battle the PQ," *Toronto Star,* October 16, 1983, p. A2.

17. *CERI Report, supra* note 5, pp. 119–120.

18. Address by Marc Lalonde, Canadian Minister of Energy, Mines and Resources, to the National Governor's Conference, Afton, Oklahoma, August 9, 1982.

19. "We've more power, gas to sell, Lalonde tells United States," *Toronto Star,* June 24, 1982, p. C3.

20. Address by Jean Chretien, Minister of Energy, Mines and Resources, to the Canadian Nuclear Association International Conference, Montreal, Quebec, June 13, 1983.

21. "Ottawa wants to boost electricity sales to U.S.," *To-*

ronto Star, October 19, 1983, p. B4.

22. "Ontario: Powerhouse for United States," *Toronto Star,* December 13, 1981, p. C1.

23. "Power Sale Studied," *Toronto Star,* August 25, 1981; Press Release, New Jersey Board of Public Utilities, August 20, 1981.

24. The MANDAN project was delayed in 1982 by a South Dakota court, but the MANDAN sponsors are pushing on. UPI Release, October 4, 1982.

25. *EIA Report, supra* note 3, p. 66.

26. "Nuclear power worth billions: Ontario Hydro," *Toronto Star,* October 4, 1981, p. A19. Ironically, in February, 1983, Environment Minister John Roberts stated that all that was needed to resolve the acid rain issue was "political will." "Roberts mocks United States 'looniness' on acid rain," *Toronto Star,* February 26, 1983, p. A1.

27. Address by Hugh Macaulay, Chairman of Ontario Hydro. "International Energy Sales—Sensitivity versus Benefits," delivered to the Canadian German Chamber of Industry and Commerce, June 15, 1982.

28. *Wall Street Journal,* December 9, 1981, p. 24.

29. "Darlington: Hydro's $12 billion gamble," *Toronto Star,* October 31, 1983, p. A17.

30. UPI release, June 11, 1982.

31. UPI release, June 20, 1983.

32. UPI release, October 12, 1982.

33. Hydro-Quebec, *Hydro-Quebec Development Plan 1983–1985: A Synopsis,* October, 1982, pp. 11, 15.

34. "Canada Considering 'Trading Company' to Handle Large Exports of Firm Power," *Electric Utility Week,* November 28, 1983, p. 1.

35. These were briefly discussed in somewhat different form in the *EIA Report, supra* note 3, p. ix.

36. Canadian National Energy Board, *1982 Annual Report,* p. 97.

37. *CERI Study, supra* note 5, p. 117.

38. Address by R.F. Brooks, Vice-Chairman of the Cana-

dian National Energy Board, before the Canadian Nuclear Association International Conference, Montreal, Quebec, June 14, 1983.

39. "U.S. Export Ban Would Cost us Billions: Hydro," *Toronto Star,* February 12, 1982, p. A8.
40. UPI release, June 26, 1981; One estimate reports Quebec's profit at $600 million per year. Newfoundland only clears $10 million per year. "The Newfoundland-Quebec power battle," *Toronto Star,* June 19, 1983, p. F7.
41. "Newfoundland loses Quebec hydro bid," *Toronto Star,* September 24, 1983, p. A7.
42. *EIA Report, supra* note 3, p. 39.
43. "Canada Trade Surplus Totaled $1.99 Billion in April for a Record," *Wall Street Journal,* June 9, 1983, p. 36.
44. Canadian unemployment recently reached 1.58 million. Over 300,000 Canadians joined the welfare rolls between March 1982 and March 1983. "Out of Work," *Macleans,* April 4, 1983. pp. 30–38.
45. "One More Push to Rescue CANDU," *Macleans,* October 11, 1982, p. 50.
46. "Trudeau in South Korea to seal Candu reactor sale," *Toronto Star,* September 26, 1981, p. A14; "Thousands of high-tech jobs hinge on Candu sale to Mexico," *Toronto Star,* December 13, 1981, p. E2.
47. "Candu contract hinges on swap of goods," *Toronto Star,* August 11, 1983, p. A8.
48. "One More Push To Rescue Candu," *Macleans,* October 11, 1982, p. 50.
49. *Id.,* p. 52.
50. Address by Jean Chretien, Minister of Energy, Mines and Resources, to the Canadian Nuclear Association International Conference, Montreal, Quebec, June 13, 1983.
51. "Hydro's risky gamble on future," *Toronto Star,* October 30, 1983, p. D1.
52. A recent editorial in the *Toronto Star* also exhorted Canadians to "push hard" on acid rain to get restrictive

controls imposed in the United States. "Let's push hard on acid rain," *Toronto Star,* June 4, 1983, p. B2.

53. Address by G.W. Nichols, New England Electric System, to the Canadian Nuclear Association International Conference, Montreal, Quebec, June 13, 1983.

54. Asinot, Richard, "Deluge," *Environmental Action,* March, 1983, pp. 12, 15.

55. *Id.* at p. 10; "Quebec's Overpowering Utility, *New York Times,* January 29, 1984, Section 3, pg. 4.

56. For example, see "Canadian Electricity May Be Cheaper, But it Doesn't Come Free of Problems," *National Journal,* May 22, 1982, p. 910; Address by Marc Lalonde, Minister of Energy, Mines and Resources to National Governors Association, Afton, Oklahoma, August 9, 1982; Address by Jean Chretien, Minister of Energy, Mines and Resources, to the Canadian Nuclear Association International Conference, Montreal, Quebec, June 13, 1983.

57. "One More Push to Rescue Candu," *Macleans,* October 11, 1982, p. 50.

58. *James Bay, supra,* note 14.

59. "The U.S. Plugs into Canadian Power," *Business Week,* May 23, 1983, p. 189.

60. Address by Jean Chretien, Minister of Energy, Mines and Resources, to the Canadian Nuclear Association International Conference, Montreal, Quebec, June 13, 1983.

61. "Ottawa wants to boost electricity sales to U.S.," *Toronto Star,* October 19, 1983, p. B4.

62. Letter from Mark D. Segal, Canadian Ministry of Energy, Mines and Resources, reprinted in *GAO Report, supra,* note 7, p. 66.

63. Address by G.W. Nichols, New England Electric System, to the Canadian Nuclear Association International Conference, Montreal, Quebec, June 13, 1983.

64. For his efforts on acid rain, Roberts was promoted to a more prestigious Ministry.

65. Frothingham, Allan. "The Liberals Sniff the Wind," *Macleans,* July 4, 1983, p. 56.
66. "Canada will cut acid rain 50% if U.S. does same," *Toronto Star,* February, 1982, p. A4.
67. UPI release, October 24, 1981. Part of this public awareness campaign apparently involved the widespread distribution of the Canadian "propaganda" movies on acid rain.
68. "Canada Tries to Organize Lobby in U.S.," *Wall Street Journal* April 12, 1983; "How we're joining the lobbying game," *Toronto Star,* April 23, 1983, p. B6.
69. One also wonders why the Canadians chose to announce their reduction in terms of allowable emissions rather than *actual* emissions. One reason may be that allowable emissions can be reduced by the stroke of a pen, while actual emissions reductions, such as those the Canadians are asking the United States to make, cost real sums of money.
70. See, e.g., National Research Council, *Acid Deposition: Atmospheric Processes in Eastern North America.* National Academy Press (June, 1983) p. 9.
71. Address by John Fraser, former Minister of the Environment, to the Izaak Walton League, Rapid City, South Dakota, June 15, 1982.
72. "U.S. stalling on acid rain Roberts says," *Toronto Star,* June 16, 1982, p. A24.
73. Even the Canadian scientific research on acid rain appears geared to headline hunting and public relations gimmicks rather than answering the genuine uncertainties which surround the acid rain issue. See, for example, "Rabbits sprayed with acid rain in test," *Toronto Star,* April 22, 1982, p. A11. In this test the rabbits' eyes were sprayed directly with concentrated acids in excess of those found in nature.
74. "Provinces willing to match U.S. acid rain reductions," *Toronto Star,* October 8, 1983, p. A12. Rather than moving unilaterally, as the federal government an-

nounced, the provinces "want to see what the Americans will do first." *Id.* This action demonstrated that, despite their effective public relations campaign, the Canadians are not the staunch defenders of the environment they would have the public believe. On the issue of asbestos standards, Canada has urged the U.S. EPA to relax the proposed American standards currently under consideration. "Cross-border rows: Canada is not always as pure as it likes to think," *Toronto Star,* October 30, 1983, p. D6.

75. "Ontario Hydro Set to Shelve Major Anti-Pollution Project," *Toronto Glove & Mail,* July 20, 1982, p. 1.

76. "Ontario lifts controls on Hydro pollutants blamed for acid rain," *Toronto Star,* February 3, 1982, p. A18.

77. "Pollution Deferral Given," *Toronto Star,* June 10, 1983, p. A7. The actions of the Province of Ontario are similar to the contradictory actions of the State of New Hampshire. In March, 1983, over 190 town meetings in New Hampshire endorsed a resolution calling for a 50% reduction in sulfur dioxide emissions. These votes received widespread publicity. Canada's John Roberts identified these votes as an "encouraging" sign in a speech to the Parliamentary Committee on Acid Rain on June 21, 1983. In April, 1983, the U.S. Environmental Protection Agency began a public comment period on a request by the State of New Hampshire to *double* its sulfur-in-oil content limitation. 48 Fed. Reg. 12109 (March 23, 1983). This action was not noted by Roberts or the media.

78. "Ottawa to allow water pollution levels double those in Ontario," *Toronto Star,* October 11, 1983, p. A1.

79. "New environment minister called 'disaster'," *Toronto Star,* August 19, 1983, p. A11.

80. Parliamentary Subcommittee on Acid Rain, *Still Waters,* October, 1981, p. 47.

81. *Id.* p. 19. Canadian sulfer dioxide emissions total 99 kilograms per person, compared with 52 kilograms per

peron in the United States. "Canada 'terrible' on acid rain: Governor," *Toronto Star,* February 8, 1984, p A3.

82. "U.S. taunts Canada on acid rain record," *Toronto Star,* February 11, 1982, p. A19.
83. "MPs vow they'll play 'hardball' to stop acid rain," *Toronto Star,* March 16, 1983, p. A19.
84. "Ottawa now gets blame for acid rain," *Toronto Star,* November 21, 1981, p. B5.
85. E.H. Pechan Associates, *Estimates of Sulfur Oxide Emissions from the Electric Utility Industry,* financed by grant from U.S. Environmental Protection Agency, (November, 1982) vol. I, p. 29–30. Ironically, those "downwind" states, which complain about midwestern sulfur dioxide emissions, increased their emissions over that same period. (Massachusetts +73%, Connecticut +27%, Maine +26%, New Hampshire +60%, Vermont +35%, Rhode Island +73%.)
86. United States Environmental Protection Agency, *The Acidic Deposition Phenomenon and Its Effects: Critical Assessment Review Papers.* Public Review Draft (June, 1983), vol. I, p. 2–70.
87. *Id.;* U.S.-Canada Memorandum of Intent, Working Group 3B. Final Report. *Emissions, Costs and Engineering Assessment* (June, 1982), p. 160.
88. Communication from official at The Cleveland Electric Illuminating Company.
89. U.S. Energy Information Administration. *Typical Electric Bills,* January 1, 1982, p. 15.
90. Address by Jean Chretien, Minister of Energy, Mines and Resources, to the Canadian Nuclear Association International Conference, Montreal, Quebec, June 13, 1983.
91. A chart of these studies is contained in Appendix III.
92. A study by the Congressional Research Service estimated that the total job loss in Ohio due to fuel switching in order to comply with an 8 million ton sulfur dioxide reduction would be between 19,200 and

21,000. In some hard hit counties, the unemployment rate would rise to the 20%–25% range. Parker, Larry, Congressional Research Service. "Mitigating Acid Rain: Implications for High Sulfur Coal Regions." May 19, 1983.

93. It should not be assumed that the high cost studies, which entail high electricity rate increases, will not result in higher unemployment even though the jobs of high sulfur coal miners will be protected. The higher electricity rates will significantly raise costs of the manufacturing industries of the Midwest, still struggling to recover from the recent recession. The study has not yet been completed which projects the job losses due to higher electricity rates in the Midwest.

94. This study was compiled and prepared for the Edison Electric Institute by National Economic Research Associates Inc. and released on June 20, 1983. Additional results are included in Appendix IV.

95. Larry Parker has written extensively on the acid rain and related issues. In the past year, at least the following studies have been released by the Congressioinal Research Service under Mr. Parker's name:

1. "Sharing the Cost of Acid Rain Control: An Analysis of Federal Financing Under H.R. 3400," September 14, 1983.

2. "Distributing Acid Rain Mitigation Costs: Analysis of a Three-Mill User Fee on Fossil Fuel Electricity Generation," April 11, 1983.

3. "Mitigating Acid Rain: Implications for High-Sulfur Coal Regions," May 6, 1983.

4. "Impact of Proposed Acid Rain Legislation on the Illinois Coal Industry," February 21, 1983.

5. "Summary and Analysis of Technical Hearings on Costs of Acid Rain Bills," July 26, 1982.

6. "Opportunities for Increased Control of Nitrogen Oxides Emissions from Stationary Sources:

Implications for Mitigating Acid Rain," December 9, 1982.

7. "Acid Rain Legislation and Canadian Electricity Exports: An Unholy Alliance?" September 15, 1982. Subsequently referred to as "CRS Study."

96. See letter from George Rejhon, Environment Counselor, Canadian Embassy, to Senator Larry Pressler, Chairman, Senate Subcommittee on Arms Control, Oceans & International Operations, and Environment. October 5, 1982.

97. *CRS Study,* pp. 6–9, 29–35.

98. *CRS Study,* pp. 24–29.

99. "One More Push for Candu," *Macleans,* October 11, 1982, p. 50.

100. *CRS Study,* p. 8.

101. Hydro Quebec, *Hydro-Quebec Development Plan 1981–1985: A Synopsis,* p. 2.

102. "Hydro-Quebec Profit Rose 4% in 1st Half," *Wall Street Journal,* August 23, 1983.

103. "Hydro-Quebec Cuts 10-Year Spending to $18.08 Billion," *Wall Street Journal,* December 7, 1983, p. 16.

104. *EIA Report, supra* note 3, p. 35.

105. *Alberta Utility Planning Council,* "Alberta Energy and Demand Forecast: 1983 to 2007," July 1983.

106. *James Bay, supra,* note 14.

107. See *CERI Study, supra* note 5, pp. 47-51. Proposed additions to Canadian generating capacity through 1990, even without dedicated exports, total over 28,000 MW. *Id.* at p. 80.

108. "B.C. nets huge sale in hydro deal with U.S.," *Toronto Star,* April 15, 1983, p. A9.

109. *CRS Study,* pp. 9-14.

110. *EIA Report, supra* note 3, p. 66.

111. *CERI Report, supra* note 5, p. 111; Address by Robert A. Hiney, Senior Vice-President, New York Power Au-

thority, to the Canadian Nuclear Association International Conference, Montreal, Quebec, June 13, 1983.

112. Address by Hugh Macaulary, Chairman Ontario Hydro. "International Energy Sales: Sensitivity versus Benefits" delivered to the Canadian German Chamber of Industry and Commerce, June 15, 1982.

113. Address by R.F. Brooks, Vice-Chairman, Canadian National Energy Board, to the Canadian Nuclear Association International Conference, Montreal, Quebec, June 14, 1983.

114. "Ohio Edison to sell excess power to GPU," *Cleveland Plain Dealer,* July 7, 1983, p. 1C.

115. "Nuclear power worth billions: Ontario Hydro," *Toronto Star,* October 4, 1981, p. A19.

116. Nastich, Milan. "Canadian Energy could lessen U.S. oil dependency," *Industry Week,* October 4, 1982, p. 13.

117. "Canada Considering 'Trading Company' to Handle Large Exports of Firm Power," *Electric Utility Week,* November 28, 1983, p. 1.

118. Canadian National Energy Board, *1982 Annual Report,* Appendix E-V.

119. *CERI Report, supra* note 5, p. 22.

120. *CRS Study,* pp. 16-17.

121. Canadian National Energy Board, *1982 Annual Report,* p. 40.

122. *CERI Report, supra* note 5, p. 114.

123. Canadian National Energy Board, *1982 Annual Report,* p. 41; "Hydro plan will double sulphur in air, Ottawa," *Toronto Star,* February 12, 1982, p. A8. "560 lakes will die if Hydro plan to export power proceeds— Copps," *Toronto Star,* December 10, 1981, p. A13; "Hydro's energy plan would kill 560 lakes, critics charge," *Toronto Star,* February 5, 1982, p. A3.

124. "Hydro deal will kill 26 lakes, MPP says," *Toronto Star,* April 16, 1982, p. A12.

125. *CRS Study,* p. 17.

126. *GAO Report, supra* note 7, p. 9.
127. *EIA Report, supra* note 3, p. 10.
128. *CRS Study,* p. 19. That is, assuming that the Canadians stick to their proposed requirements. For example, Ontario Hydro has cancelled two planned scrubbers and the Province of Ontario has relaxed stringent NOx requirements on Ontario Hydro. "Ontario Hydro Set to Shelve Major Anti-Pollution Project," *Toronto Globe & Mail,* July 20, 1982, p. 1; "Ontario lifts controls on Hydro pollutants blamed for acid rain," *Toronto Star,* February 3, 1982, p. A18. A deferral was recently given to the Algoma Steel Corp. in order to spread the costs installing of necessary pollution abatement equipment over several years. "Pollution Deferral Given," *Toronto Star,* June 10, 1983, p. A7.
129. Canadian National Energy Board, *1982 Annual Report,* p.37.
130. *CRS Study,* p.20.
131. *GAO report, supra* note 7, pp. 23, 26.
132. Recently, Cleveland Public Power purchased 6% of its supply from Ontario Hydro instead of from local coal-fired generators. Interestingly, Ontario Hydro broke off the sales after mechanical breakdowns at several of its facilities decreased the surplus available for export.
133. The *CERI Study* and others have targeted U.S. oil-fired capacity as the most likely target for displacement. See previous on transmission constraints.
135. "Ontario Hydro Set to Shelve Major Anti-Pollution Project," *Toronto Globe & Mail,* July 20, 1982, p. 1.
136. "Build nuclear plant to sell U.S. power, Ontario told," *Toronto Star,* October 25, 1981, p. A22.
137. *James Bay, supra,* note 14.
138. *GAO report, supra* note 7, pp. 10–11.
139. *GAO report, supra* note 7, p. 11.
140. Asinot, Richard, "Deluge," *Environmental Action,* March, 1983, p. 14.

141. *Id.* at p. 12.
142. "Northern U.S. States hungry for Canadian power," *Toronto Star,* June 27, 1983, p. C9.
143. "Third reactor in a week shut down at Pickering," *Toronto Star,* August 8, 1983, p. A1.
144. "Another leak discovered in nuclear plant," *Toronto Star,* September 10, 1983, p. A7.
145. "The fallout from nuclear closures," *Macleans,* November 17, 1983, p. 25.
146. "Our atomic waste feared in U.S.," *Toronto Star,* March 5, 1983, p. A12. Hoffman, Abbie, "Nuclear Waste Upstate," *New York Times,* September 27, 1982, p. A15. Canada has considered using the United States as a dumping ground for other unwanted materials. The Environmental Protection Agency is currently considering a petition by Inmont Canada to dispose PCB contaminated oil in the United States. "Denial of Canadian Petition for Disposal of PCB Wastes in United States Recommended," *Environment Reporter,* p. 1324 (November 18, 1983).